Tab. XXXI.

*CEREVS gracilis scandens ramosus    plerumq3 sexangularis, flore in-*
*genti atq3 fragranti, calyce aureo corol-    la argentea, fructu e carneo lutescente.*

J. Jac. Haid. excud. Aug. Vind.

*For Rose*

Acknowledgments

Whatever success this effort might have is due to my editor Lynne Shaner who somehow understood the importance of my teaching, compensated for the delays and still survived the pressures. No one becomes interested in botanical history and exploration *de novo*, and I owe much to Dr. LeRoy H. Hafen, the late professor of western American history at Brigham Young University who first encouraged me to write on the subject. Background research in Europe for the book was supported, in part, by National Science Foundation grant BSR-8812816.

Other titles in the Library of Congress Classics Series are:
*The First Americans* and *Mapping the Civil War*.

Designed by Cynthia Scudder

ISBN 1-56373-002-2

Printed and bound in Japan by Dai Nippon.

Library of Congress Cataloging-in-Publication Data

Reveal, James L.
    Gentle conquest : the botanical discovery of North America
with illustrations from the Library of Congress / James L. Reveal.
    p.    cm. — (Library of Congress Classics)
    Includes bibliographical references and index.
    ISBN 1-56373-002-2 : $39.95
    1. Botany—North America—History. 2. Botany—North America-
-Pictorial works—Catalogs. 4. Library of Congress—Catalogs.
I. Title. II. Series.
QK21.N6R48  1992
581.097—dc20                          92-19205
                                      CIP

*The night-blooming cereus* (Hylocereus triangularis), *native to Jamaica, was an early introduction into Europe, the cacti being an entirely new group of flowers to Old World naturalists.*

# Gentle Conquest

## THE BOTANICAL DISCOVERY OF NORTH AMERICA
## WITH ILLUSTRATIONS FROM THE LIBRARY OF CONGRESS

*James L. Reveal*

STARWOOD PUBLISHING, INC.
WASHINGTON, D.C.

# Contents

Editor's Preface.................................................5

Prologue.......................................................6

I     Old Science in a New World.......................8

II    Cabinets of Curiosities.............................20

III   The Prince and His Disciples.......................32

IV   The King's Botanist ................................48

V     Jefferson's Secretary ...............................66

VI   In Search of Magnificent Trees....................84

VII   Monuments to a Distinguished Servant.........98

VIII   Western Gold, Botanical Style ...................110

IX   Naturalists on a Disappearing Frontier........134

Epilogue......................................................156

Bibliography.................................................158

Index ........................................................159

# Editor's Preface

Third in the Library of Congress Classics Series, *Gentle Conquest* has embodied all of the challenge and discovery that we hoped for as we started this venture. The stitching together of all the pieces—the text, captions, and research—has been by turns an overwhelming challenge and a remarkable privilege.

I'll never forget the frisson that crept up my spine as our researcher Judi Chamberlain opened the first box of what would be nearly one hundred original drawings and paintings by Issac Sprague and Titian Ramsey Peale. These beautiful 19th-century illustrations are an important part of the story of western exploration; the extent of the collection was previously unknown.

We are fortunate to have found such an accomplished, witty, and delightful author in James Reveal. But in a book such as this, many people help. Thanks are due from me to Dana Pratt, Director of Publishing, and Margaret Wagner, Special Projects Coordinator of the Library's Publishing office, whose help and advice make the books spectacular; to Reid Baker and the photoduplication department, who are responsible for the outstanding photography of the material in this volume, and who helped me meet some tight deadlines. And of course, thanks to Len Bruno, Peter van Wingen, Jane Van Nimmen, Clark Evans, and Joan Higbee. And thanks, of course, Librarian of Congress James H. Billington, for allowing us to help "let the champagne out of the bottle."

—Lynne Shaner, Series Editor
Editorial Director, Starwood Publishing

# Prologue

It began five centuries ago with the "discovery" of a New World populated by a people, organized into societies and civilizations, who existed quietly in a land filled with a rich bounty of natural resources. Columbus was not the first to find this New World, nor was he the first to identify, name, and classify its flora and fauna. More than 20,000 years before, people crossed from eastern Asia into western North America. They stayed and migrated southward, balancing their demands with those of the local environment. They built cities and villages, named and domesticated plants and animals, and explored the frontier. It is mere coincidence that these people became isolated from their Old World ancestors, and mere human failing that their existence was not reported by Europeans long before 1492.

To Columbus goes the honor of being the first to effectively "discover" the New World; to him also goes the infamy of being the first to exploit its people and its natural resources.

Columbus came in search of gold, and spices, and he came in search of souls to convert to Christianity. He found far more than he could have ever imagined and gave to the New World far more than he likely wished. He found yellow gold and innocent souls, but in doing so he polluted the new land with diseases and weeds. Others would follow to accelerate the process of exploitation and final subjugation. Columbus was not alone in his actions nor, as we can see in the rain forests of the Amazon Basin, was ot the last. His was not a gentle conquest.

Yet, over the last five hundred years there has been a far more gentle conquest by naturalists searching to understand the New World's unique flora. Like the land itself, many of its plants were well known to the people who used them to feed, clothe, and heal themselves.

"Discovery" is always relative to the observer. What may be new to one may be old to another. Even the value of a discovery is relative, for what might be considered worthy, elegant, or beautiful to one might be worthless, dull, and ugly to another. The history of botanical discoveries in temperate North America is very much a story of changing fashions and desires. This history is also one that is not yet finished, as only now are scientists attempting to summarize their knowledge of the vascular plants of the region.

This is the story of great adventures, of remarkable discoveries, of brave and daring men and women, and in some cases of bitter disputes. It is also the story of our own maturation, as people and nations, resulting in an increasing appreciation of the value of plants in their natural settings. In addition to a telling of the wanderings of plant explorers in temperate North America, it is also a story of naturalists and artists working together

*Early botanical explorations in temperate North America resulted in the introduction of many elegant trees and shrubs into cultivation. The Georg Ehret illustration of the southern magnolia* (Magnolia grandiflora) *in the first volume of Mark Catesby's* Natural history of Carolina *eloquently shows the majesty of the kind of plant found by early naturalists and prized by European gardeners.*

to create beautiful botanical illustrations. Just as the natural sciences have matured over the last five centuries, so too have the talents of the illustrators and printers.

The holdings of the Library of Congress are noted for their diversity. The Library harbors some of the rarest and most spectacular of the early botanical works.

What follows is the result of five centuries in the gentle conquest of the temperate North America's botanical world.

Flos Solis maior.

# I

# Old Science in a New World

*I*t is impossible to comprehend the flora of the New World today with the eyes and minds of sixteenth-century naturalists. We are too aware of organic evolution, genetics, and ecology. We are self-conscious, and are aware that we have biases that affect the things we perceive. Their view of nature was the product of an intellectually stagnate world where for too long knowledge was confined to the classical writings of the ancient Greeks and Romans.

The Europeans who came to the New World changed it, and in doing so altered the economic and political structure of the world. Their arrival also set in motion forces that changed forever the natural sciences.

No longer would naturalists be content to accept Aristotle's view that matter consisted solely of earth, water, air, and fire, or that Theophrastos' classification of plants as trees, shrubs, subshrubs, and herbs was logical. The Middle Ages notion of spontaneous generation would prove untenable, and the belief that God provided a sign, or a "Doctrine of Signatures," for the proper medicinal use of a plant would soon be proven false.

On top of these scientific dogmas were those promulgated by Christian teachings. It was assumed that God had created the world, which was the center of the universe, and all things upon it. The number of species was fixed following the flood, and only those plants and animals saved by Noah survived. Fossils were either "figured stones" or the remains of species destroyed by the flood. By describing some 600 plants, most intellectuals thought the classical authors had accounted for all of the world's species, and there were no more to discover.

Imagine then walking through a New World rain forest knowing that there were supposed to be only six species of flowering trees with persistent, evergreen leaves. Imagine finding an animal that you had never seen or heard of, and one that, according to everything you've ever been taught, was supposed to have perished in the flood.

For the early Spanish naturalists visiting the New World or examining specimens taken to Europe, the difficulties were exacerbated by their often blind acceptance of prevailing beliefs. Some New World organisms were familiar and could be recognized, such as deer, grouse, pine, and oak, but generally none in the New World was the same as in the Old World. Worse, there were some kinds that did not quite match anything known to naturalists but still had to be fitted into the existing systems of classification and their embodied nomenclature. As a result, the American cougar became a lion and the American alligator a crocodile. But others, such as the rattlesnake, pineapple, catfish, turkey, and corn proved impossible to fit.

Could one possibly suggest that there might be new plants and animals? Were they intended for Christians?

The only option available to many early naturalists was to acknowledge that the New World contained living creatures unaccounted for by the classical scholars. These had to be given new scientific names and accounted for. This required great care so as not to offend the political and religious establishment. To avoid censure, naturalists assigned the names used (or assumed to be used) by the native people to these unknowns, and thus were merely reporting an observation rather than bringing judgment on their scientific merit. Words like moose, potato, iguana, and tobacco came into the European vocabulary this way.

*The many different kinds of squash, pumpkins and gourds seen in this 1795 illustration by Johannes Gessner were developed by native American farmers. All of these plants were unknown to Europeans.*

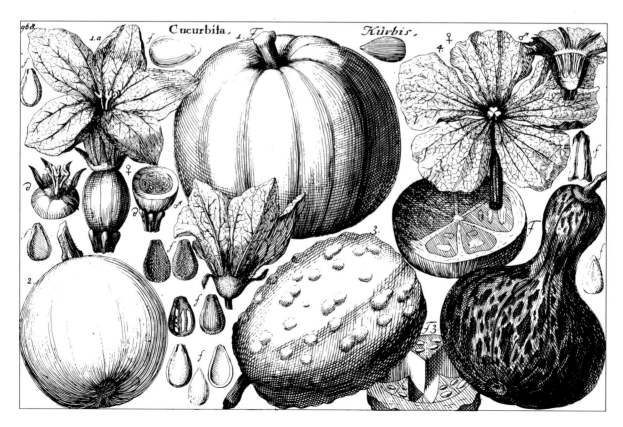

*Tobacco* (Nicotiana tabacum), *(far left) a pre-Columbian cultivated plant, became the single most important cash crop in colonial North America. Initially, Europeans considered it a medicinal herb capable of treating several diseases. The persimmon* (Diospyros virginiana), *the fruit of a small tree known to European naturalists as the "Virginia Date Plume," was eaten by Native Americans.*

Little effort was made to appreciate fully or even to acquire knowledge about the New World flora from the native peoples. Centuries would pass before it would be known that the world's largest botanical garden was then located in Mexico in a city larger than greater London. A 1552 manuscript written by two Aztecs who described, illustrated, and noted the medicinal uses of numerous species of plants would remain unpublished until 1940. An understanding of their nomenclature and their classification of plants was never even attempted by the Europeans.

The first work on the natural history of the New World was published by Gonzalo Fernandez de Oviedo y Valdés in 1526. He had traveled in the Caribbean and Central America from 1514 until about 1523, collecting natural objects and recording his observations. His *Natural history of the West Indies* was published in English in 1555, and it was this translation that attracted Sir Walter Raleigh's interest to the Americas. Oviedo struggled to fit his observations into those given in the classics and still account for an array of unique New World species of mammals, birds, insects, snakes, plants, stones, minerals, and fish as he classified the living world. He also noted, a mere thirty-some years after Columbus's arrival, the alarming number of introduced plants and animals that were becoming naturalized in the New World and the destruction they were causing. He cautioned against the Europeans' tendency to be overly dependent upon Old World species and their refusal to take advantage of local species.

Oviedo described several of the more useful American plants, noting both their potential agronomic importance and their medicinal significance. He was among the first to illustrate corn and to describe the many food preparations of cassava or manihot. In a later work, *La historia general de las Indias*, published in 1535, Oviedo illustrated pineapple and described its cultivation. He described the trees used by the Native Americans for vessels, small boats, dyes, and poisons. He knew avocado, papaya, banana, and hog plum, and he reported that guayacan was used by the Indian people to treat syphilis, a rapidly spreading disease in Europe following Columbus's voyages to the Americas.

For Oviedo, who resided in the West Indies from 1526 until 1546, the New World was a land of great natural wonders awaiting study and exploitation. For another Spanish naturalist, Nicolas Bautista Monardes, however, the New World was a vast new source of medicinal plants awaiting his personal examination. A scholar of the classics and a physician, Monardes was able to experiment with many of the New World species grown in his Seville physic garden.

His first work was published in 1569 and republished and illustrated in 1574 by Charles de L'Ecluse, the Dutch botanist. An English edition was prepared by John Frampton in the same year and given the title *Joyfull newes of the newe founde worlde*. Monardes encouraged the exploration of the New World for its medicinal wonders not only because he believed it was likely that new cures would be found, but also because of the importance of freeing Europe from its dependency on the non-Christian Far East for its most useful drug plants. A product of the sixteenth century, Monardes tended to regard most of his new medicinal discoveries as panaceas, able to cure anything. Nonetheless, he also recorded many of the Native American remedies as told to him by the Spanish so that even today his work is consulted when searching for potential drug plants.

For some, the plants and animals of the New World were not fit for Christian use for if God had intended them to be used, they would be growing in Europe. As a result, plants such as corn, potato, and tomato were occasionally regarded as poisonous or as the cause of disease. Interestingly, tobacco was not considered harmful. José d'Acosta, a Jesuit who lived in Peru from 1569 until 1588, believed that the "Heavens" did encompass the whole of the world, including the new lands to the West, and argued that plants from all parts of the world were potentially useful. In his four-volume *Historia natural y moral de las Indias* published in 1590, he concluded that the world was round and turned upon two poles or "Axeltrees." Contrary to Aristotle's beliefs, Acosta asserted that the equator was not a region of fire and sure death, nor was the opposite side of the world filled with chaos as then commonly believed. Acosta refuted many of St. Augustine's ideas of antipodes, suggested there might be a northern passage around the New World similar to the Straits of Magellan around South America, and considered the Native Americans to be descendants of Adam. Acosta believed that people migrated to the New World when the two continents were connected by a land bridge and thoroughly rejected the new fashionable notion that Native Americans were Europeans or Jewish.

More than Oviedo and Monardes, Acosta challenged the supremacy of

*In 1535, Oviedo y Valdez illustrated pineapple (*Ananas comosus*), one of the more bizarre American plants. It became highly prized by hot-house gardeners in the seventeenth century, and a favored subject of stone carvers who added its distinctive shape as an ornament on buildings and bridges.*

Pliny, Dioscorides, and Theophrastos. He maintained that these early writers were familiar only with the flora and fauna of the Mediterranean region, and, having never seen the New World, could hardly have been expected to account for its natural wonders. He chided those who still attempted to match New World species with Old World species, and argued that plants and animals in different parts of the world could be

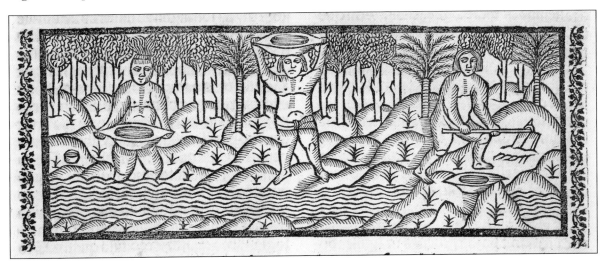

different. Acosta proposed that while all species came from Noah's Ark, "by a naturall instinct" they migrated from Mt. Ararat and found the most suitable habitat for their long-term survival. Those unable to migrate or those that remained in less suitable places "did not preserve themselves, but in processe of time perished." Extinction; a most unorthodox explanation for his time.

Acosta made only passing reference to the potato and perhaps the tomato, but he did speak of coca, the source of cocaine, and of cacao, the plant later used to make chocolate. He described the great variety of chili peppers one could find in Peruvian markets, the many uses of corn and cassava, and the assimilation of ginger and garlic, both Old World plants, into the diet of the local people.

Many of the food plants observed by the Spanish naturalists were soon in use beyond their native homes. Corn was introduced into Spain in the first decade of the 1500s, and taken to the Philippines in 1521 by Ferdinand Magellan. It was in China by the mid 1550s. The Portuguese took the plant to Africa where it quickly became a staple. In a sense, its usefulness allowed slavery to flourish more than it might have otherwise. Corn contributed to a general increase in population and filled the ships' stores while they crossed the Atlantic with human cargo.

Beans, chilies, and tomatoes, the modern foundation of any "Mexican" menu, were in common use throughout the Americas. Yet the Europeans were reluctant to adopt them. The tomato belongs to the nightshade family, and because of this, the plant was considered poisonous. Only the Italians incorporated it into their cuisine, and then not until the 1600s.

The potato, native to the high Andes of Peru, was used by the Spanish

*In early illustrations, Oviedo y Valdez (1535) showed New World agricultural practices and prickly pear (Opuntia) whose fruits were eaten by Native Americans.*

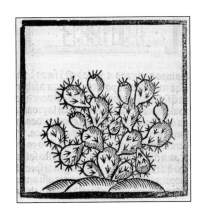

to feed sailors at sea. It was taken to Spain in the 1530s and reached Italy by 1601. In 1586, Sir Francis Drake carried potatoes from Colombia to England, stopping briefly in Virginia. For more than three centuries after that the potato was mistakenly thought to have come from Virginia. It was soon introduced by the English into the Caribbean to feed slaves, while in Europe it became a staple for the poor, providing they did not accept the prevailing belief that it caused leprosy. Like corn in Africa, the potato provided a staple food source and an increase in the population of the poor accompanied its use. It was the potato that allowed the poor to survive to become workers as the industrial revolution took form in the mid-eighteenth century, and it was the potato blight, a fungal disease that destroyed the crop in 1845, that caused widespread starvation in northern Europe and the immigration of many to the United States.

*(Above) Many groups of American plants are similar to those found in the Old World, yet different enough to be distinct. The existence (right) of new kinds of plants in the New World caused many philosophical problems for early sixteenth century European naturalists. Potato* (Solanum tuberosum) *is one of the most important of the New World crops discovered during the first half-century of European colonization. It was often confused with the tomato* (Lycopersicon esculentum). *Although both are native to South America, early naturalists believed the potato came from Virginia.*

When the New World was first visited by Columbus, botany, the study of plants, was not considered a science in its own right and neither was its most closely allied discipline, medicine. The two were joined by the fact that plants were used to treat disease and disease treatment required a knowledge of plants. Early herbals, such as Hieronymus Bock's *New Krütler Buch* (1537) and Otto Brunfels's three-volume *Herbarum vivae eicones* published the following year, were massive tomes based on the first-century writings of Dioscorides. Although Bock's work contained a wealth of details, and Brunfels' illustrated many of the species, little new was incorporated at first. With the realization that the plants from the New World, Asia, and Africa were potentially useful, these exotics were gradually accounted for in the herbals of the 1600s. Physic gardens were established, beginning in the 1550s, at medical schools and universities to aid students in their studies, and nearly a hundred different North American trees were in cultivation in European gardens by the 1630s.

In spite of Spain's premier role in the conquest of the New World, it was not in the forefront of scientific study. Indeed, that fell, as did the future of the natural sciences throughout the world, to scholars in Germany, Switzerland, the Low Countries, France, and England. Botanical gardens soon flourished in Venice, Pisa, and Florence in Italy, and in Zurich and Geneva in Switzerland. In Paris, Jean Robin and his nephew, Vespasien, grew and described several species of plants from Canada and New England in the 1590s.

While England lagged behind in these developments, it, too, soon had major gardens where New World exotics were being grown. John Gerard organized a garden on the Strand in London, another in Hertfordshire, and maintained his own in Holborn all before 1596. Robin and Gerard exchanged plants, thereby enriching both gardens. John Parkinson, a London apothecary, established a garden at Long Acre, and the medical botanist John Goodyer grew many American plants for his studies. Matthias de L'Obel, a Flemish botanist and physician who worked with Guillaume Rondelet at Montpellier in 1565, studied in England and the Netherlands before returning to England to assume the position of botanist to James I and curator of Lord Edward Zouche's garden in

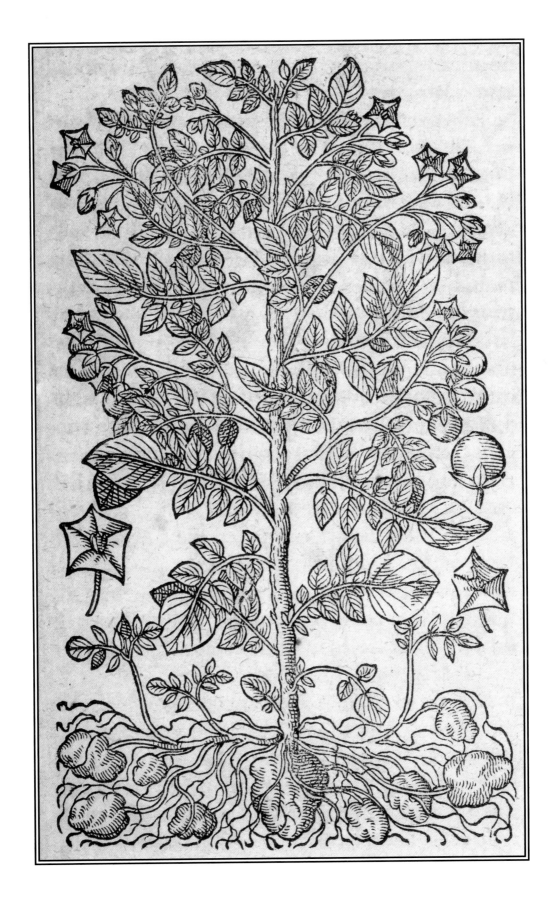

15

*(Above) An illustration of the "Doctrine of Signatures" showing how plant parts can be substituted for animal horn in the treatment of disease. Corn (*Zea maydis*), (below) a pre-Columbian cultivar, was widely planted in the New World prior to 1492. The Besler illustration of tomato (right) (*Lycopersicon esculentum*) is one of 367 woodcuts in his 1613* Hortus eystettensis, *one of the rarer books on botany in the Library of Congress.*

Hackney in 1592. Zouche is said to have invested most of his vast fortune in his garden.

Like their Continental counterparts, the English also published herbals. William Turner's 1551 *A new herball* marked the beginning of herbals in that country. Earlier, Turner had written a small book (1538) in which he named and described many British plants of potential medicinal value and noted where they could be found. Gerard, L'Obel, and Parkinson wrote their own herbals incorporating not only Dioscorides' observations, but also those made by recent authors, learned themselves or gained from others who practiced medicine in the countryside. In short, the herbal was becoming more practical. Gerard's and Parkinson's herbals, written in English, were used in the English colonies though their usefulness was lessened as the American plants were often difficult to associate with an English counterpart. The most popular edition of Gerard's herbal in the New World was its 1633 revision by Thomas Johnson; it was illustrated with more than 2800 wood-cuts.

On the Continent, gardens were rapidly becoming accepted as the symbol of wealth, power, and position. Illustrated herbals were published by the German Leonhard Fuchs in 1542 and by the Swiss Konrad von Gesner in the same year. Fuchs included illustrations of several of the New World plants growing around Tübingen among the more than five hundred species he figured. The 1554 herbal by Rembert Dodoens was translated into English by Henry Lyte and published under the title *A niewe herball* in 1578. Charles de L'Ecluse translated Dodoens' herbal into French in 1557 and then wrote a summary of the native plants of Spain and Portugal in 1576, the first major floristic work to be published.

The field of botany was now beginning to diverge from medicine. In Bologna, Andrea Cesalpino attempted to classify plants according to their physical features rather than their utilitarian value, the system of classification adopted by most herbalists. His work, *De plantis*, which appeared in 1583, was more a philosophical work than a descriptive one. He organized plants according to whether or not they had flowers and fruits, the nature of their fruits and seeds, and other morphological features. Cesalpino also collected specimens of plants that he dried and mounted on paper for permanent study. His hortus siccus of 768 preserved plant specimens is still extant and available for study.

Like the Spanish, naturalists from other European nations were constrained by their ability to make original observations in the New World. There were no organized scientific expeditions, but some individuals did report on their discoveries in works designed to promote private enterprise.

When Sir Walter Raleigh established Roanoke in 1585 he took with him Thomas Hariot (or Harriot), a mathematician and astronomer, and the painter John White. Hariot's book, *A briefe and true report of the new found land of Virginia*, published in 1588, and White's paintings, published in 1590, served to attract many new investors and colonists. Hariot traveled in both Virginia and North Carolina, reporting favorably upon the land and climate as well as describing many exotic plants and animals.

Poma amoris fructu
rubro.

Plate 2

XIV    30    31    XV    32    33    XVIII    34    35

XX 36 XXI 37    38    37    39    40    41    42    43    44    XXII    45    46    XXII    47    48

XXIII    49    50    51    52    53    54    55    56

Published as the Act directs by W. I. Ward London July 8th 1811.

So accurate were his descriptions that many species can be readily identified. Unfortunately, the observations of Captain John Smith who surveyed the Chesapeake Bay in 1608 were less critical, although his map of the region is excellent. William Wood's account of New England (1634) is a most readable account of the area, but lacks details on the natural resources.

The French, on the other hand, were more active. Jacques Cartier, in the 1530s, detailed many of the natural products of the New World, and the flora and fauna of Florida and South Carolina were described in some detail by René de Landonnière and Jacques Le Moyne in 1562. Samuel de Champlain made numerous voyages to the New World in the first two decades of the 1600s, making observations from the West Indies and Central America to eastern Canada. At Nouvelle France, near what is now Quebec, Champlain established a botanical garden where he grew Native American as well as European plants. Seeds, cuttings, and living plants were sent to the Robins in Paris. However, it was not until 1635 that the Paris physician, Jacques Philippe Cornut, illustrated several of the plants in his *Canadensium plantarum.*

In 1629, the Englishman John Tradescant and his son, known as John Tradescant the Younger, established a garden and museum at Lambeth called "Tradescant's Ark." For years, the elder Tradescant had collected plants on the Continent and in northern Africa for Robert Cecil whose father, William, had long employed Gerard. With patronage from the King and Queen, among others, the younger Tradescant traveled to the James River of Virginia in 1637 where he gathered numerous plants and animals for the museum. The garden flourished, with many of its plants providing seeds for the ever-expanding numbers of new gardens being established in Europe. Many cultivated trees today owe their origin to Tradescant's Virginia voyages in 1637, 1642, and 1654.

Plants grown in Europe from seeds gathered by Champlain, and some found by the English, were described by Caspar Bauhin in his *Prodomus theatri botanici* (1620). Bauhin thought some of the Canadian plants came from China and he termed Champlain's St. Lawrence Valley garden site "Brasiliae," causing considerable confusion about their place of origin. Garden specimens of many of the American plants were pressed and dried by Bauhin's Danish correspondent, Joachim Burser, and these specimens may still be examined at the University of Uppsala in Sweden.

Caspar, the younger brother of Johann who revised Fuchs' herbal in the 1650s and augmented it with more than 3500 woodcuts, was primarily interested in reorganizing the plant world according to their natural affinities as he understood them. His *Pinax theatri botanici*, published in 1623, accounted for the approximately 6000 species of plants then known to exist in the world. To each he assigned a single name and listed, as synonyms, names used by others in previous works. It would be this work that would be the standard for botanical knowledge for the next 130 years until it was challenged by a young man named Carl Linnaeus.

*This plate (left) from William Jowit Titford's* Hortus botanicus americanus *(1811-1812) illustrates some of the variety of New World flora, and shows the plants in relation to one another; note the corn in the center row. The North American yellow lady-slipper* (Cypripedium calceolus *var.* pubescens) *(above) illustrated by Cornut in his 1635 book* Canadensium plantarum.

*Tab. XI.*

LILIVM *folis sparsis,* *multiflorum, floribus reflexis,*
*fundo aureo, limbo auran-* *tio, punctis nigricantibus,*
*pedunculis singulis* *unico folio instructis.*

*J. Jac. Haid. excud. Aug. Vind.*

# II

# Cabinets of Curiosities

*The foremost illustrator of botanical novelties during the Linnaean era was Georg Dionys Ehret. This figure of* **Lilium superbum** *was published in Christoph Trew's* **Hortus nitidissimis.**

With the conquest of foreign lands and people came power and wealth to those Europeans willing to risk their fortunes to the fate of a ship, the success of a harvest, or the whim of a society's taste. After a century and a half of exploitation those who had sponsored the conquest were rich beyond belief. They rewarded themselves with large homes surrounded by elegant formal gardens of exotic trees, shrubs, and flowers from the farthest reaches of the known world. A man of wealth could afford to be a man of leisure, and a man of leisure was free to pursue the sciences. To this end, cabinets were filled with the curious objects of Nature's creation. To understand and tell what they had, the new rich became patrons to a host of talented men who maintained their gardens, and to those who studied, illustrated, and published great books on their holdings. It was an era of grand discoveries and an even grander display of knowledge.

Not all who sought plants necessarily craved monetary rewards. Adventurers, ships' captains and surgeons, soldiers and officers, government officials, and a host of others left the comforts of Europe for such remote lands as Africa, India, and the Americas. While most went in search of fortune, many collected strange plants for those who remained safely behind. Some did so to win favor, others to fill the time, but some were genuinely interested in the natural wonders they saw around them. And a few were even trained for the task.

Over the same 150 years, science itself underwent change. Francis Bacon argued that modern science could not be a slave to Aristotelian logic, and called for a new beginning. In 1623, Bacon suggested that science should be experimental and based on evidence derived from observations. He argued that no one person could know all. Knowledge required individually talented people working together over time with support from the state to resolve scientific questions. In England, none of the Stuarts could afford the pursuit of science as Bacon envisioned it, and his supposition that men could discover new knowledge deeply offended many religious groups. Still, in 1648, an experimental science club was formed at Oxford which, among its thirty members, included Robert Boyle and Christopher Wren. In London, a group, including John Evelyn and Robert Hooke, met at Gresham College. Both organizations came to an end with the demise of the Cromwellian Protectorate in 1659.

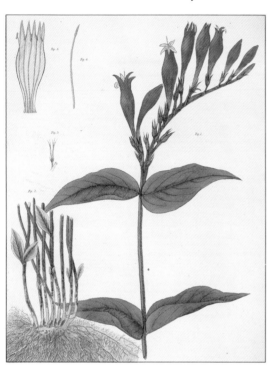

With the restoration of the Stuarts in 1660, many of the same individuals banded together to establish what Evelyn called a Royal Society. In July of 1662 a royal charter was granted by the King, and a formal organization for the promotion of experimental learning was established. By Royal decree, the new Society was not allowed to delve into divinity, metaphysics, morals, politics, or rhetoric. Across the English Channel, Louis XIV established the French Academy of Science a few months later. The Academy, unlike the Royal Society, had no patronage and was free from royal interference.

To ensure its success, the Royal Society elected to its membership not only outstanding scientists, but individuals of influence who were in a position, both within England and its colonies, to influence the direction of its scientific endeavors. Among the founders was John Winthrop, Jr. of Connecticut.

*Spigelia marilandica (above) was first collected by Hugh Jones in Maryland where the plant, native mainly to Virginia and the Carolinas, was grown for its medicinal properties. Most plants were introduced into Europe as seeds. This plate (right) from William Jowit Titford's* Hortus botanicus americanus *(1811-1812) shows the diversity one might encounter in a single shipment.*

Winthrop was catholic in his interests. In December of 1662, he presented to the Society his findings on corn. Gerard had concluded that corn had little nourishment, but Parkinson suggested the opposite. Winthrop not only supported Parkinson's conclusion, but outlined a series of additional uses corn might have, notably as a livestock feed and as a brew. His endorsement was only partially successful. Corn was widely adopted as a fodder, but human consumption in Europe did not become widespread until the Second World War.

The findings of the Royal Society were published in their journal, *Philosophical Transactions*, which first appeared in 1665. The Society not only published the new findings of its membership, but the contributions of others under the sponsorship of a member. The microscopic observations by Anthonie van Leeuwenhoek were first published in the *Transactions* in 1673. The Society also published numerous books, including Hooke's *Micrographia* (1665), Evelyn's *Sylva: or a discourse on forest-trees* (1664, 1670), Marcello Malpighi's *Anatome plantarum* (1675) and Nehemiah Grew's *Anatomy of plants* (1682).

During the formative years of the Royal Society, works were appearing without its direct support that had an impact on the acquisition of

Plate 3

Published as the Act directs, by W. J. Telford London June 1 1811.

*Lacertus*

*Styrax acerts folis.*

knowledge about the flora of temperate North America. Foremost were the writings of John Josselyn who visited New England in 1638-1639 and lived there from 1663 until 1671. His *New-England's rarities discovered* (1672) is filled with remarkable tales. He was primarily interested in the flora, and his work was the first to describe the plants from that region of North America. He estimated that there were at least a thousand new species unknown to European scientists awaiting discovery. While his illustrations were crude, even by the standards of the day, most are unmistakable. Like Hariot before him, Josselyn praised the strawberry and extolled the diversity of conifers and hardwoods available for naval stores, lumbering, and milling.

In his later work *Account of two voyages to New England* (1674), Josselyn emphasized the importance of beans, pumpkins, tobacco, and many of the small fruits such as elderberries, currants and gooseberries, and cranberries. Importantly, Josselyn also indicated what Old World species were already introduced into New England and how they were being used by both the colonists and the Native Americans. Josselyn observed the forests and remarked on the distribution of plants relative to the soil. His description of the land and the native people, as well as the social history of the New England colonists, has given Josselyn a firm place in American social history.

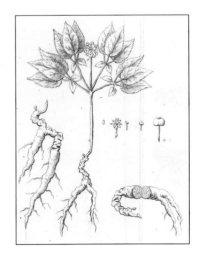

*Sweet gum* (Liquidambar styraciflua), *(left) an important medicinal plant, was an early introduction into European gardens where its aromatic balsam, called styrax, was used in perfumery. A hardy tree, it is still widely used as an ornamental.* Ginseng (Panax quinquefolium) *(above) was not used as a medicinal plant by Native Americans until French missionaries, expelled from China in the early seventeenth century, introduced the custom. Botanical specimens of ginseng were not gathered until the 1690s. A century later, thousands of pounds of ginseng roots were exported annually to China.*

The most talented of the early resident botanists in temperate North America was John Banister. Educated at Magdalen College, Oxford, and trained in the natural sciences by Oxford's professor of botany Robert Morison, Banister came to Virginia in 1678 via Barbados and other West Indian islands. He came with the support of several of the influential members of the Royal Society, including William Byrd I of Virginia. While at Oxford, Banister had collected plants at the Oxford Physic Garden, then under the supervision of Jacob Bobart and his son of the same name. Banister may have come to Virginia as a missionary for the Church of England, and if so he arrived with the support of Henry Compton, Bishop of London, whom Banister knew from his days at Oxford. Compton, a strong anti-Catholic, fell from grace in 1686 under James II and retired to Fulham Palace where he developed a magnificent garden. When restored as Bishop of London by William and Mary in 1688, Compton used his position to assign young men trained in the natural sciences to key foreign posts with the direct charge of supplying his Fulham Palace with the most elegant of species.

With the support of Byrd, the Bobarts, and Compton, Banister collected plants mainly on the coastal plains, sending bulbs, seeds, living shrubs, and trees to the younger Bobart at Oxford. Banister encountered several of the New World species gathered a half century earlier by the younger Tradescant. Many of Banister's plants were studied and illustrated for Morison's *Plantarum historiae universalis oxoniensis*. In return, Byrd received European plants from Bobart, which were grown in Virginia.

Banister soon entered into a correspondence with England's most respected natural scientist, John Ray. In 1684, Ray encouraged Banister to collect all he could and to name the new species. Four years later Ray published, in an appendix to his *Historia plantarum*, Banister's "Catalogo plantarum seipso in Virginia observatarum" wherein Banister named many new species.

Many of the members of the Royal Society were interested in botany, and they, along with others, met informally at a coffee house forming the Temple Coffee House Botany Club. The membership encouraged the

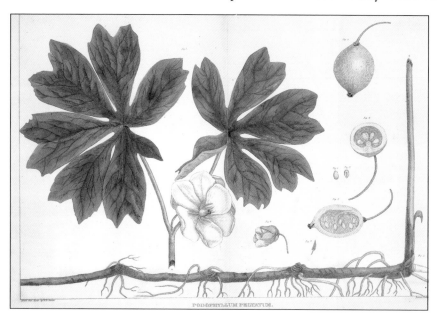

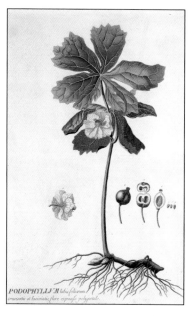

*Mayapple* (Podophyllum peltatum) (above) *was long regarded as a medicinal plant, and early introduced into Europe for its properties. Even today, the drug podophyllum is an important compound in the development of anti-cancer drugs.*

*The tulip tree* (Liriodendron tulipfera) (right), *so named because of its tulip-like flower, was once common in the forests of eastern North America. Its fine, soft, white wood was used extensively in cabinetry by American colonists.*

collection of plants in foreign lands, their propagation locally, and their scientific study. Banister was one of the Club's more productive contacts. After 1688, Banister was sending specimens and illustrations of the plants he was finding to London. These were examined by various members of the Club, but none was more interested than Leonard Plukenet.

Ray's leading rival in scientific botanical matters was Plukenet, a rather ill-tempered man of dubious virtue. He and Ray competed to be the first to describe new plants from around the world. By 1688 Banister was proposing to write his own natural history of Virginia, which he wished to illustrate. Morison had published illustrations of a few of the American plants in 1680, but Ray's *Historia plantarum* lacked figures. Unfortunately, Morison had died in 1683, and Ray was finding it difficult to publish a third volume. Plukenet was planning his own summary of the world's flora, which he proposed to illustrate. The problem was that few of his colleagues at the Temple Coffee House Botany Club were willing to allow him access to their cabinets of curiosity or to their gardens.

Nonetheless, Plukenet obtained Banister specimens and sketches from the Bishop of London and from the Keeper of the Chelsea Physic Garden, Samuel Doody. Today, Plukenet's bound volumes of dried plants preserved in The Natural History Museum in London contain numerous Banister specimens. Likewise, many of the illustrations in Plukenet's *Phytographia*, which he began publishing in 1692, are copies of Banister's sketches.

Tab. X.

Virga aurea Marilandica, spicis florum racemosis, foliis integris, scabris.

Hermanno Boerhaave
A. L. M. & M. D.
In Academia Lugduno-Batava
Botanices, Chemiae & Medicinae
Professori.

Van Huysum pinx.

F. Kirkall fe.

Banister's sudden death in a shooting accident on an expedition with Byrd to the Roanoke River in May of 1692 abruptly ended the Botany Club's ready access to American plants. Almost at once a replacement was sought, and the task fell to George London. A letter to Edward Lhwyd, Keeper of the Ashmolean Museum at the University of Oxford, brought a potential candidate.

The Ashmolean had become the resting place of the Tradescants' collections in 1679, and was, by the 1690s, the best museum in Great Britain. Lhwyd had in his charge a Welsh student who had "no skill at all in plants" but who could be made "a fit man to succeed Mr. Bannister" with a little effort. The young man was Hugh Jones.

After a few months of intensive training, and a rushed ordination by Compton, the newly made minister-naturalist set out for Maryland to promote the faith according to the Church of England and to collect plants for the good Bishop of London and his Temple Coffee House friends. Jones arrived in Maryland in 1696 and set to work on his dual charge. His patron, the Royal Governor of Maryland, Francis Nicholson, quickly realized Jones was unfit as chaplain and assigned the young man to Christ Church Parish in Calvert County. Away from the colony's capital, Jones was able to collect, but with neither Banister's skill nor freedom.

In November of 1697, William Byrd II moved that the Royal Society "think of a Fitt person to be sent over to Virginia." This time, William Vernon of St. Peter's College, Cambridge, was called upon to travel to America to collect. Once again, Francis Nicholson came forth with the funding and Vernon headed for Maryland rather than Virginia. But Vernon was not the only naturalist heading for America in the late winter of 1698.

One of the members of the Botany Club was the London apothecary James Petiver. Petiver was quickly amassing the largest collection of dried plant specimens then in existence. Most foreign collectors sent their specimens to Petiver, a voluminous correspondent. Petiver had secretly arranged for Jones to send him and Doody the plants from Maryland; it was little wonder that Compton and George London were dissatisfied with Jones's efforts. To protect his interest in the Maryland flora, Petiver dispatched his close friend, the physician David Krieg. Thus, in 1698, Jones, Krieg, and Vernon were all botanizing in Maryland.

The results were impressive and overwhelming. Krieg and Vernon collected up and down Maryland's Chesapeake shoreline, and Jones

*John Martyn's* Historia plantarum rariorum, *(left) published in 1728, was one of earliest works with color-printed plates. The figures are engraved on copper plates by J. van Huysum. Seeds of this goldenrod (*Solidago altissima*) were sent to Collison by Richard Hill of Londontown, Maryland. Virginia bluebell (*Mertensia virginica*), (above) found by Banister, was first cultivated in the gardens of Henry Compton, the Bishop of London. It was reintroduced by John Custis in 1747.*

increased his efforts in Calvert County. But with the sudden reassignment of Nicholson to Virginia in the fall of 1698, Vernon's patron left Annapolis and Vernon departed for London. Krieg, who had sailed on another ship so as not to compete directly with Vernon, also returned to England. After shipping his specimens to Petiver, Jones remained behind, now suffering from the first indications of the tuberculosis that would kill him in the early winter of 1701.

In England, there was an immediate scramble for the plants. Vernon presented Compton with a share, with another going to Hans Sloane, the powerful secretary of the Royal Society and a noted botanical collector. Krieg's specimens went to Petiver and Doody; Petiver in turn gave Sloane a full set of Krieg's plants. Sloane sent his Maryland specimens to Ray for naming, and Doody gave his to Plukenet. The race was on to see who named them first!

Plukenet immediately turned his attention to the new plants, and had several illustrated. Ray, on the other hand, ill and in his seventies, complained bitterly of their poor state. Petiver, too, began to publish several of the new species, illustrating a few as he provided new names. Between them Ray, Plukenet, and Petiver proposed nearly 700 new scientific names. Altogether, Jones, Krieg, and Vernon gathered more than 650 different kinds of plants in Maryland, or about a quarter of the colony's flora. Plukenet published his new names in 1700 and 1705, with Ray's volume appearing in 1704. But the first to publish was James Petiver whose first article on Maryland's plants appeared in the November, 1698 issue of the *Philosophical Transactions*.

*John Banister of Virginia collected the spotted* Monarda punctata *(above) in the 1680s, but the plant was best known to Linnaeus from garden and herbarium specimens gathered by John Clayton in the 1730s. This illustration was published by James Edward Smith who purchased Linnaeus's herbarium and library in 1784. One of the first North American flowering trees (right) introduced into Europe was the dogwood* (Cornus florida).

The death of Hugh Jones in 1701 brought an end to organized collecting in the English colonies. Although the younger Byrd once again tried to bring a collector to Virginia, there was little interest in doing so. Trees from Canada and New England had been in European gardens since the mid-1500s; Tradescant had brought many of the Virginian species into cultivation in the 1640s. First Banister, then Jones, Krieg, and Vernon had completed the task. The fickleness of the English gardener had shifted from the trees and shrubs of the New World to those of China. James Cuninghame, surgeon for the East Indian Company in China, had sent to Petiver a wealth of curious plants, some 600 in all, which revealed the even greater diversity of flowering trees and shrubs in that part of the world.

China was the new Eden. For a while, it was botanical quiet in Virginia.

Pl. 48.

P. J. Redouté del.

Gabriel sculp.

Dogwood.

# III

# The Prince and His Disciples

*Shall Britons,*
*in the field unconquer'd still,*
*the better laurel lose?*
*In finer arts and public works*
*shall they to Gallia yield?*
  ROBERT JOHN THORTON (1807)

Kalmia angustifolia, *sheep*
*laurel. This romantic*
*illustration is from Thornton's*
*Temple of Flora, 1807.*

*C*arl Linnaeus, Swedish-born naturalist, teacher, physician to the Queen, and self-promoter, proved to be the one person capable of rendering sense from nonsense in the botanical world. In recognition of his own accomplishments he crowned himself the "Prince of Botany." History would prove him correct. Botany, by the mid 1700s, was beginning to separate into its modern disciplines. With medicine removed, although most practitioners still earned their university degrees in medicine, botany was predominantly taxonomy—the identification, naming, and classification of objects, and Linnaeus was its acknowledged leader.

Prior to Linnaeus, and especially prior to 1753 when he published *Species plantarum*, plants were given long, multi-worded Latin phrase names (polynomials) such as "Chrysanthemum Marilandicum, caule & foliis hirsutis Hieracii, flore magno, pluribus petalis radiato, disco granti protuberanate." Linnaeus simplified this to *Rudbeckia hirta*, a two-word name (binomial) consisting of a one-word generic name and a one word specific epithet, still in Latin, the universal language of scholars. Linnaeus also decided that each species should have one, and only one, scientific name, and that name should be adopted by everyone as long as the name was appropriate and placed in the correct genus.

Linnaeus reduced the nomenclatural chaos created by previous authors by basically ignoring their names. He also ignored past efforts to classify plants into "natural" groups, and it would be this latter notion that would eventually result in the collapse of Linnaeus's own "sexual system" of classification.

Linnaeus's success lay in his enormous energy and personal charm. He was also successful because he was able to convince certain key naturalists in Holland, France, and England that his approach was both correct and, more importantly, practical. Through them and his students he obtained specimens and books on botany from throughout the world, allowing him to amass a large library and herbarium. From his many friends Linnaeus received a steady flow of new and previously unknown plants, both as specimens for his herbarium and as seeds and living plants for his garden. He sent his students to Africa, China, and the New World. Lone naturalists in remote places gathered objects of curiosity for the great Linnaeus in the hopes that they too would be honored by him with a new generic name.

To the English and Dutch, Linnaeus was a new god. He summarized all of the genera of plants he believed worthy of scientific consideration and proceeded to organize them so anyone could identify and name them. At the pinnacle of his career he accounted for all of the species in each genus he felt worthy of recognition. The chaos he inherited was no more, and the Linnaean disciples followed him faithfully.

That would be the future; getting there would not be easy.

As Linnaeus rode the coach to Oxford from London in August of 1736, his reputation as the new savior of systematic botany preceded him to a skeptical John Jacob Dillenius. German-born, Dillenius had come to England in 1721 at the invitation of William Sherard, professor of botany at Oxford who, in spite of his position, resided in London. Dillenius had gained fame for his work on cryptogams, mainly lichens and mosses, and was asked by Sherard to assist him in the preparation of a new edition of Bauhin's *Pinax*.

Dillenius found an active botanical community in London. The seemingly ageless Sir Hans Sloane dominated the scene, both by his position in the Royal Society as secretary and eventually president, and by his wealth. He bought the cabinets of curiosity of many of his friends as they died, notably Leonard Plukenet and James Petiver. While Sherard, through Morison at Oxford, acquired a large herbarium when he became professor, Sloane's collection was by far the largest and most complete.

The *Pinax*, as conceived by Bauhin, was an attempt to summarize all knowledge regarding the scientific names of plants. The manuscript Dillenius obtained from Sherard was only partially completed because of Sherard's inability to gain access to the Plukenet and Petiver specimens then in Sloane's possession. Sloane and Sherard had a long-standing quarrel which, it was hoped, Dillenius could bridge. In London, Dillenius worked through the literature, consulting many of the rare botanical volumes in Sherard's library. Unfortunately, Dillenius was no more successful with Sloane than was Sherard, and when Sherard died in 1728, the manuscript was still unfinished.

In Sherard's will, he stipulated that Oxford could obtain his herbarium and library if the University made suitable provisions to maintain them. He was also willing to endow a professorship if Dillenius was selected as its first recipient. The conditions were accepted. In time, Sherard's library of some 600 volumes and his large collection of dried plants were given to

*The insectivorous northern pitcher plant,* Sarracenia purpurea *(above) and the purple wake-robin of North America,* Trillilum erectum *(right) were known to European naturalists since their introduction in the sixteenth century. Both were highly prized as ornamentals.*

Trillium erectum.

T. 69.

*Rana Terrestris*          *Sarracena*

Oxford, and Dillenius took up residence at Oxford as the first Sherardian Professor of Botany in 1734.

The delay was caused by James Sherard, William's brother. He challenged provisions in the will, and induced Dillenius to concentrate on a book describing the plants of his garden at Eltham. The publication of *Hortus elthamensis* in 1732 caused a further delay in Dillenius's compilation of the *Pinax*, but it did allow him to formally describe several new species from southern Africa and eastern North America.

*T*he source of most of the new American species, however, was Mark Catesby. Born and educated in Essex, England Catesby went to Virginia in 1712 at age 29. At Williamsburg, where he lived with his sister and her husband, he became acquainted with Governor Alexander Spotswood and met William Byrd II. Almost immediately, Catesby began to collect seeds that the governor sent to Henry Compton and dried specimens that Spotswood sent to Samuel Dale, who had inherited John Ray's herbarium. In 1715, Petiver published a note on Catesby's Virginia plants, including several from the western mountains. When Catesby briefly went to Jamaica and Bermuda in 1714, he collected plants and sent them to Sloane. Dale shared his specimens with Sherard who, in 1717, had returned to England after serving fourteen years as the British Consul to Turkey at Smyrna. When Catesby returned to England in 1719, he brought with him more dried specimens, which he gave to Dale. Dale was impressed by Catesby and urged that he be encouraged to return to Virginia. In October of 1720, Francis Nicholson, now about to assume the royal governorship of South Carolina, informed the Royal Society that he would sponsor Catesby if the Society would approve Catesby's appointment. With the support of Sloane, Sherard, and a dozen others, Catesby arrived in Charles Town, South Carolina, in May of 1722 to begin a new era of botanical exploration in that colony.

James Petiver had continued to encourage his American correspondents to send him plants after Maryland's Hugh Jones died in 1701. For him, some of the most exciting discoveries came from the Carolinas, Georgia, and Florida. Edmund Bohun of Charles Town, his neighbor Robert Ellis, and ship's captain, William Halsteed, sent seeds and living plants to Petiver, while Hannah Williams provided him with numerous new species of butterflies, snakes, scorpions, lizards, shells, and a few plants. One of the best collectors in the first decade of the eighteenth century was Joseph Lord, a 1691 graduate of Harvard College and minister who, in 1695, settled in South Carolina. Williams encouraged Lord to collect plants, and in 1701, his first efforts were sent to Petiver. After that, Lord sent specimens to Petiver on a yearly basis, providing him with detailed remarks on their use by Native Americans and on their natural settings. In turn, Petiver described many of the new species, sharing seeds and living plants with his London friends.

To the north, and with the encouragement of Halsteed, John Lawson collected plants in North Carolina for Petiver. Lawson was a surveyor, and

*The plants in some of Catesby's illustrations are difficult to identify. The figures are poorly executed and the colors are dubious. The leaf at the left is probably a crude depiction of* Sarracenia minor. *The flower and leaf on the right is probably* Sarracenia flava, *although some recent authors have suggested it might be the hybrid known as* Sarracenia x Catesbaei.

STUARTIA Malacodéndron.

when commissioned Surveyor-General of North Carolina in 1709, he was able to travel widely in the colony collecting numerous specimens. Unfortunately, in 1711, Lawson was killed by Tuscarora Indians who "stuck him full of fine small splinters of torchwood, like hogg's bristle, and so set them gradually on fire."

Catesby found the hospitality of Charles Town most conducive to his scientific efforts. As a complete naturalist, he collected, drew and water-colored many of the plants and animals he found in the three years he spent traveling from North Carolina to northern Florida. The botanical specimens he sent to England were fought over by Sherard and Sloane, but sets went to Dale and several of the Continental botanists as well. Catesby's seeds and living plants were grown in many gardens, and in turn, Catesby received exotic species that he introduced into the Carolina gardens of his neighbors.

In 1725, Catesby sailed to the Bahama Islands, bound for England, having failed to convince his patrons that he should concentrate his future efforts in Mexico. He spent a year on the islands and returned to London in 1726. Upon his return, Catesby sought support to publish his scientific findings, but little was forthcoming. With a loan from the Quaker woolen-draper and horticulturalist, Peter Collinson, who was gradually taking the place of the deceased James Petiver as botanical correspondent to the world, and employment in the various nurseries, Catesby was gradually able to publish his *Natural history of Carolina, Florida and the Bahama islands*. Engraved and colored by Catesby himself, with the exception of the *Magnolia grandiflora* plate done by Ehret, the plates were generally accurate. Dillenius aided him in identifying his plants and in providing the new species with suitable names. In 1733, Collinson presented Catesby to the Royal Society and he was duly elected.

*The spectacular flowering shrub,* Stewartia malacondendron, *was found near Williamsburg, Virginia, by John Clayton who sent specimens to Gronovius. Gronovius, in turn, sent a portion of the collection to Linneaus who proposed the name in 1753. The species is rare today in the Williamsburg area.*

Catesby's plants and his publication were two of the reasons Linnaeus was traveling to Oxford. A third was Sherard and Dillenius's unfinished revision of Bauhin's *Pinax*. In 1735, Linnaeus had published *Genera plantarum*, his attempt to provide a single, correct name to each genus of plants then known in the world. Now, in 1736, Linnaeus was thinking of trying to account for all the known species, and to tackle that task required the kind of information Dillenius had in his manuscript.

Linnaeus, born in 1707, left his native Sweden in February of 1735, traveling to Holland. He had asked for the hand of Sarah Lisa Moraea, but her father demanded that young Carl obtain his medical degree from a foreign university and be apart from his daughter for a least three years. In Holland, Linnaeus quickly obtained his degree at Harderwijk University (it took a week), and was soon visiting Holland's best known naturalists, Herman Boerhaave, Jan Frederik Gronovius, and Johannes Burman. Through Boerhaave, Linnaeus was employed by the wealthy Amsterdam banker, George Clifford, who had a large estate near Haarlem, Hartecamp.

The gardens at Hartecamp were large and rich in species; Clifford also had an extensive library and a cabinet of curiosity. Linnaeus's tasks at the estate were to serve as Clifford's physician and to catalog the botanical collections. Living "like a prince," as Linnaeus said, and free to devote all of his energy to the study of plants, he published many books filled with novel ideas on how plants should be classified and named. An encyclopedist in an era of encyclopedias, Linnaeus was able to digest great amounts of information and restate it in a clear, concise form.

Clifford insisted that Linnaeus travel to London to study the great collections then owned by Sloane, speak with Dillenius, and indirectly obtain as many rare plants as he could for Clifford's estate.

For eight days Linnaeus visited Dillenius at Oxford, walking in the botanical garden, looking at specimens in the herbarium, and talking. By the end, the once-dubious Dillenius was offering to share his professorship with Linnaeus if only the young Swede would remain in England, and wept when the coach left returning Linnaeus to London.

*Poison-ivy (*Toxicodendron radicans*) was one of the first temperate American plants recognized by naturalists, not only because it represented a new group of plants, but also because of the rash it causes when it comes in contact with skin.*

At Oxford, Linnaeus examined the collections of Catesby. It is not known if the two men discussed John Clayton of Virginia. Clayton had recently sent Catesby a large collection, but because he was concentrating on his own *Natural history*, Catesby sent it on to Gronovius in the hope Gronovius would name the plants. A few of the Clayton specimens had been retained at Oxford, and some of the seeds taken by Collinson, but the majority of both were in the hands of Gronovius by the fall of 1735. It is likely that Linnaeus reviewed many of Catesby's specimens while at Oxford in order to identify the Clayton material, which he was hoping to study upon his return to Holland.

When the Clayton family came to Virginia in 1705 the family was in disarray. The botanist's grandfather, Sir John Clayton, and his father, John, had been accused of absconding with a substantial portion of the estate of Sir Jasper Clayton who died in 1660. For some fifty years, the conditions of his will were fought by Sir John's sister, Prudence, in a long series of lawsuits. It is not known where Sir John went when he departed England, but his son, John, leaving his young family behind, went to Virginia where he settled in Williamsburg.

Trained as a lawyer, John Clayton quickly found a position as secretary to the newly appointed lieutenant-governor, Edward Nott. He rose rapidly in prominence, serving as an assistant to the attorney general in 1707, becoming a member of the College of William and Mary in 1710, and attorney general in 1713. Two of his sons, Arthur and John, probably came to Virginia in 1715. The Claytons lived in Williamsburg and enjoyed the friendship of Virginia's elite and all of the city's advantages.

The younger John was also educated in law and in 1720, at the age of 26, he assumed the post of Clerk of the County Court for Gloucester County, a position he held for 53 years. In 1723, John married Elizabeth Whiting, the daughter of Major Henry Whiting, who owned Elmington, a large plantation along the North River. The Whitings were a family of considerable wealth, and because the tithe payable to the Clerk of the County Court was considerable, John and Elizabeth lived in comfort at their new home, Windsor, along the Pianketank River.

THE UNIVERSAL POWER OF LOVE.

MOTTO.

Hence,— in bright leaves the sexual pleasures dwell,
And Beaux and Beauties crowd the blossom's bell,
With meeting lips and mingled smiles they sup
Ambrosial dew-drops from the nectard cup:

Delighted Hymen marks their whispered vows
And binds his chaplets round their polished brows,
Guides to his altar leads the flowery bands,
And as they kneel unites their willing hands.

*Another of the romantic illustrations in Thornton's 1807* Temple of Flora, *this depiction of Hymen and sexual love as the forces behind floral propagation indicates the tendency toward anthropomorphism popular at the time.*

It is likely that John Clayton became interested in botany through his contact with Mark Catesby. Clayton was probably among the "Knights of the Golden Horseshoe," as the young men who accompanied the 1716 Spotswood expedition to the Blue Ridge were called, when Catesby botanized in that part of Virginia. The two corresponded, but it was not until the spring of 1734 that Clayton began to collect botanical specimens with the idea of sending them to Catesby for identification. Catesby was working on his *Natural history* and perhaps needed more material of certain species, or perhaps he recognized the need for someone to collect in the colony, but for whatever the reason, Clayton spent the winter of 1734-1735 working up his small collection of perhaps a hundred

*(Above) This illustration, opposite the title plate of Nickolalus Joseph Jacquin's* Selectarum stirpium americanarum historia, *(1763) shows new world plants and gives an interesting look at the European view of native Americans. The close relationship among Linnaeus, his correspondents and their collectors is reflected by this illustration (right). Linnaeus named the northern horse-balm Collinsonia to honor his Dutch patron George Clifford who provided funding for publication of* Hortus cliffortianus. *The plant was drawn by Georg Ehret and grown from seeds John Bartram sent to Jan Frederik Gronovius in about 1735.*

specimens. The following summer they were sent to Catesby, and by November they were in the hands of Gronovius.

Probably using the library of William Byrd II at Westover and the parts of Catesby's work then published, Clayton attempted to identify and classify his collection following the methodology established by John Ray. Gronovius, already impressed with Linnaeus's new method of classification, reworked many of the specimens, sending the new genera to Hartecamp where Linnaeus was completing the text for his *Hortus cliffortianus*. Equally impressed with both the novelty of the new finds and their preservation, Linnaeus asked to see more. Meanwhile, Clayton continued to collect, sending more than a hundred additional specimens in the summer of 1736 and perhaps as many as two hundred specimens in 1737.

Linnaeus spent the winter of 1737-1738 at Leiden with Gronovius. With the 1737 shipment, Clayton sent a manuscript catalog of the Virginia flora that Gronovius, with Linnaeus's aid, completely rewrote following the new Linnaean method. Instead of telling Clayton what he was doing, Gronovius wrote Catesby, as "the custodian of the temple of the American Apollo," in the hopes that Catesby would inform Clayton that he would soon be publishing a *Flora virginica*. No letter seems to have reached Gloucester County, so Clayton never learned the fate of his manuscript until he read the introduction of Gronovius's 1739 *Flora*.

Despite this plagiarism, Clayton continued to collect plants and send them to Europe.

It was obvious to Catesby and to Collinson in England that if Clayton was to write his own flora of Virginia he had to learn the Linnaean methodology. This was also understood by Clayton who asked for as many of Linnaeus's books as they could obtain for him, as well as other works on botany. In 1738, Clayton sent two large trunks of seeds and specimens, but in May of that year Linnaeus left Holland for France where he visited the great botanical garden at Paris, and by September was in Stockholm asking for the hand of the waiting Sara Lisa. Nonetheless, duplicates of Clayton's Virginia plants were soon on their way to Linnaeus. He wished the world's foremost botanist, as all now recognized Linnaeus to be, to bless each with a name so that they might appear in a second part of the *Flora*. More specimens followed in 1739, 1740, and 1743.

In November of 1738, Clifford presented Gronovius with several copies of Linnaeus's *Hortus cliffortianus* with instructions to send one to Clayton. When Clayton received the book in the spring of 1739, he found, for the first time, many of his new plants named and described.

One, spring beauty, then in flower near his home, was to henceforth bear the scientific name Claytonia.

After Gronovius published *Flora virginica* in October of 1739, Clayton became convinced that if he was to be given credit for his own efforts, he had to prepare his own manuscript for publication. Clayton was rapidly learning the new way of characterizing and classifying plants, and his own observations, still being sent to Gronovius, were now more precise. Clayton was also able to correct errors long embedded in the literature, and to clarify some relationships among various groups of plants. When a second part of *Flora virginica* was published in the late fall of 1743, Clayton vowed to begin his own publication.

*The cross-vine* (Bignonia capreolata) *was known to Linnaeus from illustrations published as early as 1674, sometime after the plant was introduced into Europe, possibly by John Tradescant the Younger.*

Clayton was not able to devote all of his energies to botany. His court duties took considerable time, and his family was expanding as well. The youngest brother, Thomas, arrived in 1727 and established a medical practice in Gloucester. Clayton's brother Arthur died in 1733, and in 1737, the elder John Clayton died at the age of 72. Two years later, Thomas died, his wife said, of "overwork." These years were a period of both sadness and great fortune. The elder Clayton had resolved the legal difficulties in England in 1726, and had acquired considerable property in Virginia as well as in England. All of this came to his son, John. The small plantation of some 450 acres was productive, the price of tobacco relatively stable, and John Clayton was, more than ever before, in a position to buy botany books and find the time to travel in search of plants.

In 1743, Benjamin Franklin and nine other Philadelphians established the American Philosophical Society, modeled after the Royal Society in London. Clayton became a member in 1744. Also admitted to membership was Clayton's fellow Virginia botanist, Dr. John Mitchell, who resided at Urbanna along the Rappahannock River north of Gloucester. He came to Virginia in 1735 and remained until 1746 when illness forced him to return to England. He corresponded widely with many naturalists, including Linnaeus. Mitchell was interested in a broad array of subjects, and knowledgeable in most judging from his many writings. He began sending Virginia plants to Europe in 1738, and based his comments on the specimens now at Edinburgh, he already possessed a number of botanical works in his personal library. In 1742, Mitchell sent a long manuscript to Collinson describing several new genera of Virginia plants; with the manuscript was a collection of 560 plant specimens. Publication was delayed until 1748, and by then many of his new genera were found by Clayton and described by Linnaeus. Nonetheless, Mitchell's 1748 paper contained information on ten new genera.

Of greater importance were Mitchell's comments regarding the concept of a species as a basic unit of classification. For many authors, such as Morison, Ray, and Plukenet, species were often poorly defined subunits of a genus and established as much to denote geographic location as to state morphological differences. While the French naturalist, Joseph Pitton de Tournefort, did much to resolve the question of "what is a genus" in a work published in 1700, he did little to resolve the species problem. Likewise, Linnaeus's own *Genera plantarum*, published in 1737, further refined the definition of what constituted a genus, but "what is a species" remained vague.

To most, naturalists or not, a genus was a logical division of nature. The genus was a group of related organisms that shared a series of similar morphological, or structural, features. What Tournefort had shown in 1700, and Linnaeus reinforced in 1737, was that floral characters, rather than vegetative features, were the most reliable indicator of generic relatedness. Tournefort, however, felt that all of the floral features taken together should be considered when determining whether or not a previously unknown plant represented a new genus or was merely another species in an already established genus. In this way, related genera could be associated into natural groupings, similar to those recognized by Ray, and today termed families. Linnaeus objected. While he accepted Tournefort's views on the definition of genera, he felt that the genera should be arranged into groups based on the number of reproductive parts in the flower. This became known as Linnaeus's sexual system.

The revolution Linnaeus started was the stabilization of the genus and the ease by which anyone could classify (and identify) any plant. Anyone who could count the number of stamens and pistils in a given flower could place it in one of Linnaeus's twenty-four classes. By reading a series of terse, diagnostic phrases, one could then arrive at a group of genera. From there, one had to review the diagnostic features of each of the included genera to find the one to which the plant belonged. Most of those diagnostic features were based on the fruit.

Linnaean genera were more broadly defined than those of Tournefort, and thus easier to identify. His genera were arranged in artificial groups that could be easily understood. Tournefort's genera were more narrowly defined, and thus more numerous, and his were arranged in natural groups defined by a series of complex morphological features that were not always easy to understand, let alone observe.

The problem at the species level was much more complex. Linnaeus

*Chelone obliqua was named by Linnaeus in 1762. The only specimen seen by him was collected by either John Bartram or John Clayton. The original collector of many of the specimens used by Linnaeus to establish scientific names can not now be established. Only by knowing who was collecting, and where they were searching for plants, can one speculate on the original source of a given specimen.*

and Tournefort could easily define the genus Geranium, but as to the number of species, there was little agreement. Tournefort recognized seventy-eight species, Linnaeus thirty-nine, and several of those were not known to Tournefort in 1700. The prevailing view was that all the world's species had been created at one time and it was merely the role of humans to recognize these creations. Species were a stable unit in nature, propagating themselves without change. For Linnaeus it was merely a matter of finding the essence of the plant to understand its position in nature. He was enough of a nominalist to realize that his understanding was limited to only those plants that he knew, and with each new discovery, his understanding of the essence of a group could change. Linnaeus sought to analyze nature apriorially, whereas Tournefort and his later followers were more inductive.

The contribution Mitchell made that was so fundamental to the understanding of species was his view that species should be defined biologically. Members of the same species, Mitchell argued, ought to be able to freely cross and produce prolific offspring. Members of the same genus might be able to cross and produce offspring, but these would be sterile. Plants that were unrelated would not be able to produce any offspring. Likewise, in classifying plants, it was Mitchell's view that all the attributes of a plant, not just its flower or fruit characteristics, must be considered.

Clayton and Mitchell discussed their views of nature, but to Clayton, these were too esoteric; what he should do was concentrate on the discovery of new plants—let the philosophical arguments be waged by others. Mitchell's interests were too broad for Clayton who was struggling just to stay abreast of the developments in botany. Mitchell, on the other hand, was equally at home making observations on such widely various subjects as: animals; resolving the "Causes of the different Colours of People in different Climates"; practicing medicine; and writing papers on the treatment of disease, notably yellow fever.

By the late summer of 1745, Mitchell was so ill that he sold his Virginia property, including his scientific books, and in the early spring of 1746, surrounded by boxes of specimens, set out for England. On the crossing, Spanish pirates boarded the ship and took his collections, including more than a thousand specimens of plants. Mitchell arrived in London destitute and discouraged, his botanical career essentially over.

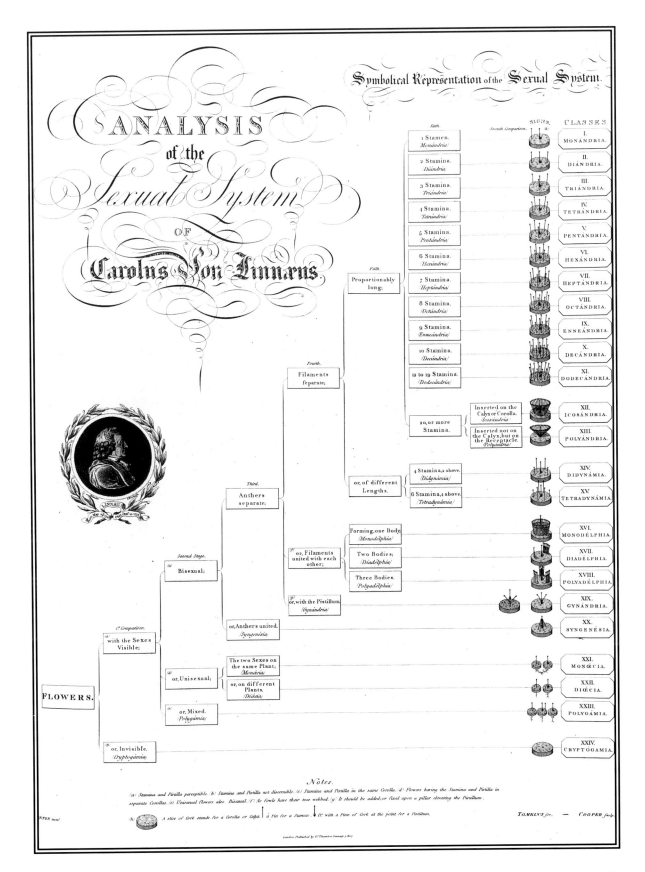

Symbolical Representation of the Sexual System.

ANALYSIS
of the
Sexual System
OF
Carolus Von Linnæus.

| | | SIGNS | CLASSES |
|---|---|---|---|
| Sixth. | Seventh Comparison. | | |
| 1 Stamen. (Monándria) | | | I. MONÁNDRIA. |
| 2 Stamina. (Diándria) | | | II. DIÁNDRIA. |
| 3 Stamina. (Triándria) | | | III. TRIÁNDRIA. |
| 4 Stamina. (Tetrándria) | | | IV. TETRÁNDRIA. |
| 5 Stamina. (Pentándria) | | | V. PENTÁNDRIA. |
| 6 Stamina. (Hexándria) | | | VI. HEXÁNDRIA. |
| 7 Stamina. (Heptándria) | | | VII. HEPTÁNDRIA. |
| 8 Stamina. (Octándria) | | | VIII. OCTÁNDRIA. |
| 9 Stamina. (Enneándria) | | | IX. ENNEÁNDRIA. |
| 10 Stamina. (Decándria) | | | X. DECÁNDRIA. |
| 12 to 19 Stamina. (Dodecándria) | | | XI. DODECÁNDRIA. |
| 20, or more Stamina. | Inserted on the Calyx or Corolla. (Icosándria) | | XII. ICOSÁNDRIA. |
| | Inserted not on the Calyx, but on the Receptacle. (Polyándria) | | XIII. POLYÁNDRIA. |
| or, of different Lengths. | 4 Stamina, 2 above. (Didynámia) | | XIV. DIDYNÁMIA. |
| | 6 Stamina, 4 above. (Tetradynámia) | | XV. TETRADYNÁMIA. |

Fifth. Proportionably long;

Fourth. Filaments separate;

Third. Anthers separate;

(f) or, Filaments united with each other;
- Forming, one Body. (Monodélphia) — XVI. MONODÉLPHIA.
- Two Bodies; (Diadélphia) — XVII. DIADÉLPHIA.
- Three Bodies. (Polyadélphia) — XVIII. POLYADÉLPHIA.

(g) or, with the Pistillum. (Gynándria) — XIX. GYNÁNDRIA.

or, Anthers united. (Syngenésia) — XX. SYNGENÉSIA.

Second Stage. (c) Bisexual;

1ˢᵗ Comparison. (a) with the Sexes Visible;

(d) or, Unisexual;
- The two Sexes on the same Plant; (Monœcia) — XXI. MONŒCIA.
- or, on different Plants. (Diœcia) — XXII. DIŒCIA.

(e) or, Mixed. (Polygámia) — XXIII. POLYGÁMIA.

(b) or, Invisible. (Cryptogámia) — XXIV. CRYPTÓGAMIA.

FLOWERS.

Notes.

(a) Stamina and Pistilla perceptible. (b) Stamina and Pistilla not discernible. (c) Stamina and Pistilla in the same Corolla. (d) Flowers having the Stamina and Pistilla in separate Corollas. (e) Unisexual Flowers also Bisexual. (f) As fowls have their toes webbed. (g) It should be added; or fixed upon a pillar elevating the Pistillum.

(h) ⬤ A slice of Cork stands for a Corolla or Calyx. ⫮ a Pin for a Stamen. ⬤ Dᵒ with a Piece of Cork at the point for a Pistillum.

THORNTON invᵗ. TOMKINS fec. — COOPER sculp.

London Published by Dʳ Thornton January 3 1807.

47

48

# IV

# The King's Botanist

Castby, Clayton, and Mitchell were not the only discoverers of curious plants from temperate North America who worked with Linnaeus. To the north, others were sending specimens and in time, Linnaeus would send one of his students to collect American plants. But throughout Linnaeus's long career, which lasted from 1735 until 1778, one man, John Bartram of Philadelphia, continually sent him new and exciting plants.

Born in Darby, Pennsylvania, in 1699 of Quaker parentage, John Bartram was raised from an early age by his grandmother and an uncle following the death of his mother and the departure of his father for North Carolina. In time Bartram married, and had two sons, one of whom died in infancy. Following his wife's death in 1727, he purchased a farm along the Schuylkill River about three miles from Philadelphia. He remarried in 1729, and started a new family that eventually numbered nine children. At this time he laid out a five-acre botanical garden. The garden, eventually operated by John Jr., and supplied with specimens by another son, William, dominated their lives for nearly a century.

Bartram's interest in botany was always practical. He was first concerned with medicinal uses of plants. From his Quaker friends who were scholars or had gardens, he gradually learned the more technical aspects of plant structure, classification, and identification, and he began to search for plants to bring into cultivation. In 1729, his friends presented him with a copy of Parkinson's *Paradisi in sole paradisus terrestris* that required him to hone his skills in Latin. When London's Peter Collinson urged the Philadelphia merchant Joseph Brientnall to send him plants, Brientnall countered by recommending Bartram.

Collinson was soon writing to Bartram with specific requests. Bartram was told how to make dried specimens for study, how to gather seeds and fruits, and how to prepare them for safe transportation to London. Finding a person willing to respect his instructions, Collinson was soon supplying Bartram with collecting supplies, field equipment, books on natural history, a compass, and even clothing.

Bartram soon realized that if he collected seeds in the woods and meadows of Pennsylvania, and planted them in his own garden instead of sending them directly on to London, he could accomplish several goals not mentioned directly by Collinson but obvious to Bartram.

If he collected only a few seeds of any one species in the field, then he could collect seeds of more species. By planting them in his own garden, he could not only increase their numbers, he could select seeds from those individuals that did best in cultivation. As a result, the seeds, cuttings, and young living plants Bartram sent to Collinson were superb. In addition, Collinson sent European seeds to enrich Bartram's own garden, and in turn, Bartram was soon selling garden plants to others in the Philadelphia area. By early 1736 Bartram's contributions were so appreciated that Collinson and others in England were providing Bartram with an annual allowance of ten guineas to promote his botanical efforts.

Collinson realized that he had found a skilled provider of American plants, and gave Bartram's plants to a very select group. Specimens were going to Sloane to enrich his vast collection of dried plants. Seeds and specimens were going to Dillenius at Oxford, but it was the flowering trees, shrubs, and wild flowers that were slowly filling the vast garden of Lord Petre that were making the most important impression.

Robert James, the eighth Baron Petre of Writtle, Essex, was an enthusiastic botanist, and although only in his early twenties, he had built a large garden at Thorndon Hall, near Brentwood, where about 10,000 American trees and shrubs were mixed with about 20,000 others from Europe and Asia. His gardener was James Gordon, and the botanical touch that would serve him well for nearly half a century had its origin with Catesby and Bartram plants at Thorndon Hall.

With Lord Petre as a patron, Collinson was able to secure the support of others, including Charles Lennox, Duke of Richmond. In 1737 Bartram planned a botanical foray of some 1,200 miles from Pennsylvania southward through Delaware and Maryland to Virginia. Armed with Collinson's instructions, including a warning "that thou not appear to disgrace thyself or me," and several letters of introduction, Bartram set out in the spring of 1738, visiting many of Collinson's American correspondents.

In Maryland, Bartram sought out Dr. Richard Hill of Londontown on the South River who had supplied Collinson with seeds of Maryland plants since the 1720s. A few of Hill's plants were illustrated by the Cambridge botany professor John Martyn in his *Historia plantarum rariorum.* Bartram visited the plantations of John Custis—whose widowed daughter-in-law married George Washington—and William Byrd II. He also visited Clayton's home, but his fellow naturalist was off collecting, and it would not be until 1760 that the two men would actually meet.

*Pl. 11.*

H<sup>h</sup> Redoute del.        Renard sc.

ILEX opaca.

When Dillenius accepted the position at Oxford, one of his goals was to complete his work on the lichens and mosses of the world. He called upon Collinson to encourage all of his correspondents to collect these small, non-flowering plants. Clayton sent several examples from Virginia. Bartram sent Collinson and Dillenius hundreds of specimens, all carefully wrapped and labeled. For Dillenius, Bartram's specimens were a refreshing change from the routine and common specimens most collectors sent him. Bartram seemed to find mosses in the most unexpected places, so that Dillenius soon came to appreciate the diversity of these small plants in temperate eastern North America. Even after Dillenius published *Historia muscorum* in early 1742, in which he illustrated many of the new species Bartram found during his 1738 travels, Bartram continued to "crop" mosses and send them on to London.

*T*n 1742, Bartram traveled up the Hudson River to the falls of the Mohawk River, collecting plants in the Catskills and visiting Cadwallader Colden at Coldengham. Colden, a trained physician, had long ago laid aside his practice to concentrate upon business and politics. Colden first settled in Philadelphia in 1710 and practiced medicine there, but in 1720 he was appointed Surveyor General of New York and moved to that colony. He became a leading figure, ultimately serving as Lieutenant Governor (1761).

His interests in the sciences were broad. He had been encouraged to collect natural objects by James Petiver in 1709, had discussed botany with James Logan while in Philadelphia, and had written *The history of the five Indian nations of Canada* in 1727 thereby improving European understanding of the indigenous people. He speculated most successfully in land, and in 1728 built a country estate near Newburgh, New York, that he named Coldengham. There he raised his family, cultivated a garden, and entertained a growing number of America's resident naturalists.

When Bartram arrived in 1742, Colden was already well known to Collinson in London and Gronovius in Leiden. Through his European correspondents, Colden built an extensive library. He had just obtained a copy of Linnaeus's *Genera plantarum*, and was attempting to master it when Bartram arrived and the two men discussed the merits of Linnaeus's sexual system of classification. Bartram urged Colden to collect plants locally, and within a year Colden was sending specimens and descriptions to Collinson. In January of 1744, Colden wrote to Linnaeus with a proposal to prepare a catalog of the plants near Coldengham. By December, he was writing Gronovius pointing out some of the faults in Linnaeus's methodology and calling for the development of a more "natural" system.

Colden's manuscript entitled "Plantae Coldenhamiae in provincia Novaboracensi Americanes sponte crescentes" was published in two parts (1743, 1749) by Linnaeus who was editor of the Swedish journal *Acta Societates Regiae Scientiarum Upsaliensis*. Unfortunately, the dried specimens sent by Colden to voucher his catalog were taken

*The American mountain ash (Sorbus americana) (left) was described by John Bartram's cousin Humphrey Marshall in 1785 in* Arbustrum americanum, *an alphabetical catalogue of the forest trees and shrubs native to the American portion of the United States. A map of the coastal Carolinas (above) south to northern Florida in William Bartram's 1791* Travels.

by the same Spanish pirates that took John Mitchell's Virginia plants in 1746, and they were never recovered.

Following the loss of his collection, Colden's energy for plant collecting lessened considerably, and soon he even tired of exchanging seeds.

*Sarracenia rubra (above) was described by Thomas Walter of South Carolina in 1788. Conrad Loddiges who introduced many American plants into England and published illustrations of several in his series* The botanical cabinet *included the plant among his two thousand hand-colored figures.*
*A John Bartram seed catalog (right) from the Library of Congress Broadside Collection.*

For Linnaeus, the years after leaving Holland were filled with a variety of duties. He married Sara and in time three children were born into his household. He moved upwardly professionally, assuming a professorship at the University of Uppsala, filling the position once held by Olaus Rudbeck. In a letter to a colleague, Linnaeus wrote "Thank God I have been freed from my miserable medical practice in Stockholm."

His project to summarize all of the species of plants in the world, however, was not so promising. The early effort in Holland was thwarted by his inability to study critical specimens, especially those held in the jumbled herbarium of Sir Hans Sloane. At Collinson's request, Sloane made some effort to logically arrange his materials, but he did not promise to open his collection for others to study. Once Linnaeus became established in Uppsala, he again took up the challenge.

By now Linnaeus had a firm understanding of the genera. New editions of *Genera plantarum* appeared with some regularity. When he wrote *Hortus cliffortianus*, Linnaeus had attempted to account for each and every name applied to each species as he understood them. This was proving to be an impossible task. Others were actively describing new species from all over the world, and while he was receiving their publications, specimens—so critical for a full understanding of a species—were not always readily available.

In 1747, Linnaeus resumed the task of compiling a world's flora to the species level. He labored on the project well into 1748 before illness, duties, and a chaotic household rendered the venture more one of frustration than fulfillment, and he gave up. He completed about half the manuscript. Linnaeus was a man of great energy and able to work rapidly, but he was also subject to periods of depression manifested in admissions of scientific impotence and failure. His own frankness and absolute belief in his own correctness made him dogmatic to some and therefore subject to criticism; which both frustrated and annoyed Linnaeus.

Life at Uppsala was, nonetheless, rewarding. His works were hailed throughout the world. Specimens were sent to him for comment, and often to be named. He received honors both national and foreign. His many students filled his rooms, drank his beer, annoyed Sara, and took his time. He worked long hours, slept little, and eventually built a small stone building in the garden for his collections where he could get away from everyone.

Many of Linnaeus's students were traveling abroad and sending him material from strange, new lands. Through his association with the Count of Tessin, he and Magnus Lagerström, director of the Swedish East India Company, made it possible for many naturalists to visit the Far East. To North America, however, Linnaeus sent Pehr Kalm.

Kalm came to Philadelphia in 1748, having spent several days in London, including a pleasant afternoon with Mark Catesby and John Mitchell. In London, Kalm also met Collinson, who suggested he seek out John Bartram who, Collinson assured him, would take care of his every need. In September, Kalm was received by Bartram and Benjamin Franklin, and he spent the fall of 1748 collecting plants in Pennsylvania

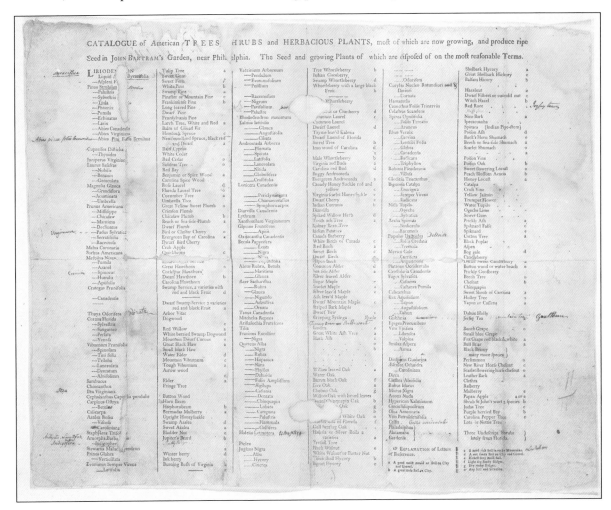

and New Jersey. In 1749, Kalm traveled through New York to the St. Lawrence Valley of southern Canada, collecting wherever he went, and returning to spend the winter in Philadelphia. The following year he went westward, through Pennsylvania to Niagara Falls and Oswego, before going back to Bartram's garden laden with dried specimens and seeds. In February of 1751, Kalm sailed for England where he remained for a month, reaching Uppsala in June.

The winter of 1750-1751 had been kind to Linnaeus. While bouts with depression were more frequent, he had managed the winter without serious illness, and the spring had been warm. When Kalm arrived at Linnaeus's home, the former student brought an array of new and exciting specimens, numerous seeds, and warm greetings from many of Linnaeus's friends.

*Illicium floridanum.*

Kalm had kept a diary and he wanted to publish it forthwith and include the names of the plants. Accordingly, he asked his mentor to name them. To what extent this spurred Linnaeus into action is not known, but to fulfill this request meant that he had to account for all of the new species. A man not known to waste his time, Linnaeus apparently felt that to properly name the new American species he should return to his task, and account for all species worldwide as well.

*The Florida anise-tree*
(Illicium floridanum).

The success of *Genera plantarum* was that by sheer scholarship Linnaeus had forced upon the world one, and only one, name for each genus. These names were given according to a series of familiar principles newly outlined in his *Philosophia botanica* published in Stockholm in December of 1750. He reasoned that the same concept should be applied to species as well; each species, no matter where it occurred naturally in the wild, should have one and only one correct scientific name. And who, other than Linnaeus, could give each plant such a name?

Taking up his discarded 1747-1748 draft, Linnaeus composed the first sixty-seven printed pages of *Species plantarum* in just eight days. By November of 1751, Linnaeus had completed the first volume and, in July of 1752, the entire text of more than 1200 pages was done. He had given up the hope of ever resolving the nomenclatural nightmare of accounting for all previously published names and contented himself with listing only those he could resolve himself. Species he did not know or species proposed by authors he did not trust simply were ignored. But most importantly, Linnaeus hit upon the notion of assigning each species in a genus a one-word epithet. That word would be unique within the genus, although the same epithet might be used in other genera. Thus, in 1753, when *Species plantarum* was published, Linnaeus named sixty-three species for Virginia, each in a different genus.

In North America the desire to find a new species did not cease simply because Linnaeus had presented the world with its first floristic summary. As long as there was a botanical frontier there would be new objects of interest to discover. The race now was to get each novelty named and described following the new Linnaean methodology. It was generally accepted that the first person to ascribe a name to a new plant would have that name accepted by all others. Henceforth, priority of publication became important.

For those who remained secure in the comforts of Europe, importance lay not only in who named the plant first but how it was classified. For nearly forty years, from 1753 until 1789, textbooks, articles, and pamphlets flooded the market promoting Linnaeus's sexual system with scores of drawings showing even the most casually interested person how to identify any plant they cared to examine.

New American collectors did their part in this effort. A transition was taking place in the field of North American botany. Pehr Kalm, with the first part of his *En resa til Norra America* published in 1753, was soon professor of natural history at Åbo. The death of Mark Catesby ended his distinguished career. Also, at age ninety-three, Sir Hans Sloane died in 1753. His passing and the appearance of *Species plantarum* defined the end of one era and the start of another.

*L*eft to carry on the task of exploring temperate North America for its botanical wonders were John Clayton and John Bartram, men now nearly in their sixties. Three new names were quick to make their appearance onto Linnaeus's American scene, two the offspring of others who had already contributed to *Species plantarum*.

In 1754, the elder Bartram took his fourteen-year-old son William with him on a collecting trip to New York. At Coldengham there was a fortuitous meeting of the next generation. Although the elder Colden had given up his interest in botany nearly a decade earlier, the Colden household was still botanically active, for the tasks of exploring, identifying, drawing, and classifying plants had been taken up by his daughter Jane. William, who was already recognized as a skilled illustrator, was also drawing many of the plants he was seeing on his travels. The third member of the threesome was Alexander Garden, newly arrived from Charles Town, South Carolina, and already an active collector of the local flora.

Garden had arrived at Charles Town in April of 1752. The city and countryside were in full bloom and the diversity of plants immediately caught his attention. He soon discovered that no one, save a few slaves, knew the plants or anything about them. From a friend, Dr. William Bull, Garden obtained a copy of *Flora virginica*, and while that helped sóme, many of the plants were still unknown. Bull also gave Garden a variety of Linnaeus's smaller works, including *Fundamenta botanica* (1736), a forerunner to *Philosphica botanica*, from which Garden learned the Linnaean methodology by dissecting more than a thousand different plants.

One of the plants Garden studied was Indian pink, a medicinal plant of some importance in the treatment of intestinal worms. Catesby had put the plant in the genus *Solanum* while Linnaeus had placed it in *Lonicera*. From Garden's own dissections, he was certain that both were incorrect and felt the plant belong to a new genus. Garden proposed to name it *Huxhamia* for the London physician Dr. John Huxham who had promoted *Cinchona* as a cure for fever. Garden sent Huxham an account of the plant's virtues and its description in 1754, which Huxham read before the Royal Society. In 1767, Linnaeus acknowledged his error and established *Spigelia marilandica*, the name Indian pink is known by today. Interestingly, the only Maryland collection of this plant ever found was gathered by Hugh Jones in the 1690s.

The spring of 1754 found Garden collecting along the coast as far south as northern Florida, gathering all kinds of strange plants and animals when illness overtook him. To avoid the summer heat, Garden went to Coldengham.

In 1754, Garden was all of 24 years of age, Jane Colden five years older, and William Bartram a decade younger. The three became good friends.

*John and William Bartram found franklinia in 1765 on a bluff near the Altamaha River near Fort Barrington, Georgia. Marshall suggested* **Franklinia alatamaha** *in 1785, naming the genus in honor of "that patron of sciences, and truly great and distinguished character, Dr. Benjamin Franklin." The tree, last found in the wild in 1803, was probably rendered extinct by the Bartrams and others who introduced it into cultivation.*

Tab. XXII.

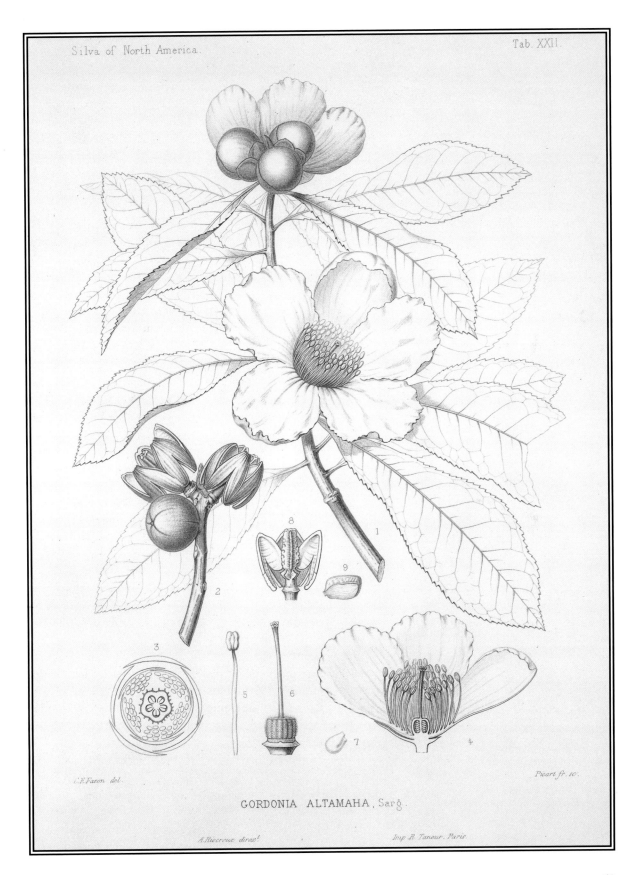

C.E.Faxon del.

Picart fr. sc.

GORDONIA ALTAMAHA, Sarg.

A.Riocreux direx.<sup></sup>

Imp. R. Taneur, Paris.

Soon Jane had penned Gardenia for a plant she felt was a new genus, and Garden, having promised the Bartrams he would soon visit them in Philadelphia, was leisurely collecting plants and minerals in the Catskills.

The small scientific community of Philadelphia immediately welcomed Alexander Garden into its midst. He visited with the governor, discussed the American Philosophical Society with Franklin, and marveled at the Bartram garden. Instead of sailing south, Garden decided to ride overland, despite the rough November weather, with the primary purpose of collecting seeds. He now had the names and addresses of the important European botanical contacts: Gronovius, Collinson, and Linnaeus. Not about to waste their time with trivial matters, he would send them only the most exciting of the strange and curious.

Dionæa muscipula.

*The Venus fly trap was collected in 1762 by William Bartram who took the plant to Philadelphia. He reported its Native American name to be "tippitiwitchet." William Young took live plants to England in 1768, and one of these, in flower, was examined by John Ellis. Ellis published* Dionaea muscipula, *named for the Goddess of Beauty, in a gentlemen's newspaper,* The St. James's Chronicle, *in September, 1768.*

For Jane Colden, the five years that were to remain in her life were filled with home duties gladly interrupted by her botanical labors. Her manuscript grew, each new dissection adding more information, each new sketch more finely executed. Yet her death in 1759 would render her a forgotten figure, her manuscript ending up in the Natural History Museum in London and not published until 1963, long after its scientific usefulness was gone.

As for Garden, he also felt forgotten and most assuredly ignored. His careful studies were revealing many mistakes in Linnaeus's *Species plantarum* which he was calling to the attention of Collinson and another Englishman, John Ellis. As Collinson aged, Ellis was becoming Linnaeus's new intermediary in London. Through Ellis, Garden sent several specimens to Linnaeus he regarded as new species and genera. Ellis, who was mainly interested in coral, encouraged Garden by telling him that any new genus he found would be illustrated by the great Georg Ehret.

In 1755, Garden accompanied Governor James Glen on an expedition in the Cherokee land, serving as physician. Near Saluda, where the Governor met the Cherokee and ceded them several hundred square miles on behalf of the crown, Garden collected a small tree that he recognized as a new genus. This he named Halesia, for the Reverend Stephen Hales, author of *Vegetable staticks*, an early work on plant anatomy. Garden sent Ellis specimens and seeds, which were immediately planted and germinated the following year (1757).

The plant had been found by Catesby and illustrated by him, but his description was faulty, and Linnaeus did not account for it in 1753. When Ellis asked for more seeds, Garden was unable to return to the mountains, and instead rode northwest of Charles Town to the banks of the Santee

River where he gathered seeds. Meanwhile, Ehret drew the plant Garden originally found, and a copy of the unfinished plate was sent to Linnaeus who acknowledged that it was a new genus and agreed to name it for Hales. This Linnaeus did in his 1759 *Systema naturae*, calling the montane shrubs *Halesiâ carolina*. Ellis, who by now had received the new seeds from Garden, set out to write his own description of the plant from the Santee River, naming it *Halesiâ tetraptera* in 1761. For more than two hundred years, the two names were confused, and their true origins and identity were not unraveled until 1976.

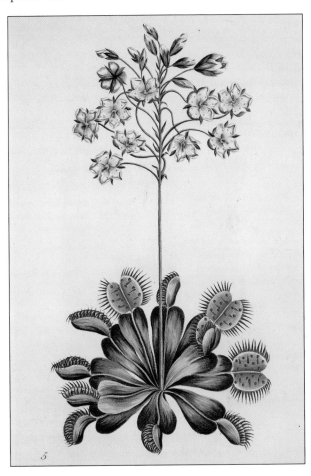

*M*eanwhile, Garden was lamenting all of the other new species that Linnaeus was ignoring. When John and William Bartram stopped in Charles Town to visit Garden on their way to northern Florida in 1760, all three were discouraged by Linnaeus's inattention to their findings. Even John Clayton, whom the Bartrams had visited a few weeks earlier, was disappointed having never fully recovered from the ill-treatment Gronovius had shown him by publishing all of the new Virginia plants under his name rather than Clayton's.

Clayton, at least, was busy trying to resolve his situation. With the encouragement of Collinson, Clayton had been drafting a new flora for Virginia, and Ehret was preparing illustrations for the expected publication. Still, Collinson delayed publication, and the fact that Clayton was still working on the manuscript did not help.

Linnaeus had accounted for many of Bartram's new species in the same work in which Halesia was published. Golden seal or yellow root, a medicinal plant found in the forests of Pennsylvania and Maryland, had been named *Hydrastis canadensis*, and the native eastern tumbleweed was named *Amaranthus albus*. Garden had been pleased by the publication of *Calycanthus floridus*, the sweet-shrub, which he had found near Saluda, and Ehret had illustrated in 1755. Even a few of Clayton's newer collections were proving to represent new species which Linnaeus was giving names.

For young William, the future was bright indeed. Garden offered to take him as an apprentice; Franklin suggested William become a printer. Collinson approved of the latter, but all agreed that while William's education at the Academy in Philadelphia was first rate, his first loves were botany and art. Already William's drawings of birds were being used by George Edward in his *A natural history of uncommon birds and gleanings of natural history*, which Linnaeus used to name formally many American

*This plate, from John Hill's* A decade of curious and elegant trees and plants *(1773) is a lovely, but innacurate, illustration of the Venus fly trap. The flowers are much too large, and the perfectly arranged lower foliage can be found nowhere in nature. The illustration opposite shows the maturation of botanical illustration over time, as it appeared in Loddiges* Botanical Cabinet *forty years after Hill's publication.*

species. William's father was concerned more for his young son's future than his happiness, and in 1756 apprenticed him to a Philadelphia merchant.

In 1761, William joined his father's half brother, William, at the latter's trading post on Cape Fear in North Carolina. At the same time, John botanized along the Ohio River with Colonel Henry Bouquet and explored the forests from the Shenandoah Valley southward to South Carolina in 1762. By now he was collecting fossils and animals as well.

*B*artram's eyesight had long been failing, and while Franklin's new invention, bifocal eyeglasses, helped at first, Bartram realized his collecting days were numbered. When Britain obtained Florida from Spain in 1763, he declared to Collinson that botanizing in Florida was his next goal. However, it remained secondary to his quest to be appointed King's botanist, and Bartram asked his London friend to once again marshal support before the Court. To everyone's great surprise, William Young Jr., an immigrant German nurseryman from Philadelphia, was named Botanist to the King and Queen in 1764 and awarded a yearly sum of £300. Young, who was in England at the time, returned to America in 1766 and collected plants mainly in the Carolinas. He returned to England in 1768, presenting to the British Museum some 300 water color drawings. His only publication, a 1783 catalog of American plants, did not adopt Linnaean nomenclature and was published in Paris. His name was misspelled as "Yong" on the title page, and today is known only from a few copies. His contributions were sadly inferior to Bartram's. Finally, in 1765, thanks largely to Collinson, the elder Bartram was finally appointed King's botanist, but awarded only £50 per year for his efforts.

In June of 1766, William joined his father at Charles Town, and after exchanging pleasantries with Garden, the Bartrams set out for St. Augustine, Florida. The trip was notable for the many new species of plants they found, and the fact that in February of 1768, Collinson, on behalf of Bartram, presented his first box of plants to the King. Shortly afterwards, Collinson died, and it remained for Franklin to present the second box in the months prior to the start of the American Revolution.

Meanwhile, William was back in Florida, collecting all he could find that was new and exciting. From 1773 until 1777, William collected throughout northern Florida, Georgia, and the Carolinas. He sent many of his seeds and dried specimens to England where they were incorporated into a new botanical garden at Kew, southwest of London. Like his father, who published his adventures under the title *A Description of East Florida* in 1766, William also kept a diary, eventually publishing his *Travels* in 1791.

John Bartram died in 1777. The American colonies were at war with England, and old associations were being strained. Franklin had asked that Bartram send his specimens to Paris, but none could be gathered. When Gronovius published a second edition of *Flora virginica* in 1762, Collinson told Clayton he could no longer champion a new Virginia flora

*Canna* Flaccida     *Balisier* Flasque

in London; perhaps, Clayton was told, he might find a publisher in America. The manuscript and Ehret drawings were sent to Clayton, but no publisher was found, and interest in the flora died with Clayton in 1773.

*T*he fates would continue to be unkind to Clayton and his memory. His own collection, manuscript, and the Ehret plates were lost when the British burned the Gloucester County Courthouse. His personal library and correspondence were lost in a house fire around 1906, and today, the exact location of his home, Windsor, once situated along the Pianketank River, is no longer known. Sadly, no one since Gronovius has written a flora of Virginia.

Linnaeus, too, passed from the scene. His death in 1778 was heralded as a great tragedy. Gone was the one person who knew the world's flora, the one person who maintained stability and resolved conflicts in the field of plant taxonomy. Within a decade the French tore at the fabric of the Linnaean method, and while some in England tried to maintain his artificial system of classification, others felt a more natural system was called for.

This debate, which would rage until 1830, was largely fought by gentlemen in dinner dress or scholar's robes. It was followed, albeit casually, in the newly declared United States. There the urge was not to resolve some theoretical problem but to explore the great and ever expanding western frontier for its scientific curiosities. And no one was more interested in this pursuit than the third president of the United States, Thomas Jefferson.

*The Atamasco lily* (Zephyranthes atamasco) *by Pierre Joseph Redouté, one of 486 plates of liliaceous plants published in eight volumes from 1802 until 1815. The plates are hand finished, color-printed stipple engravings.*

# V

# *Jefferson's Secretary*

*Bitterroot, the state flower of Montana, was named* Lewisia redivia *by Frederick Pursh in 1813 in honor of Meriwether Lewis, President Jefferson's personal secretary and co-leader of the Lewis and Clark Expedition to the Pacific Ocean from 1804 until 1806.*

Thomas Jefferson was a frustrated man. For more than two decades he had been trying to get naturalists to explore the vast western part of the American continent. As early as 1783 Jefferson had tried to convince Revolutionary War hero George Rogers Clark to lead an expedition. Three years later in Paris, where Jefferson was serving as the minister to France, he became acquainted with John Ledyard, a Connecticut Yankee with wanderlust. Jefferson suggested that Ledyard travel across Russia to Kamchatka, and cross over to Nootka Sound aboard a Russian vessel. From there, Ledyard would walk east to Virginia. He was game, but Empress Catherine objected, and Ledyard was turned back in Siberia.

A more realistic and promising proposal was put forth in 1792. The French botanist André Michaux submitted a proposal to the American Philosophical Society for a scientific expedition to the Northwest Coast of western America. Jefferson, then Secretary of State, had urged Michaux to make his proposal, and then supported it not only within the Society but without as well in an effort to obtain £3600 to fund the expedition. The Society accepted the proposal in April of 1793, but in December of 1796, the project was abandoned. In the intervening years, much had happened.

Michaux had been trained by Bernard de Jussieu, whose concepts of a natural system of classification were in direct conflict with the sexual system of Linnaeus. He had worked with Jean Baptiste de Lamarck, the author of a major botanical encyclopedia and *Flora française*, and collected plants in Persia from the Caspian Sea to the Indian Ocean from 1782 until 1785. Michaux first came to America in 1785, setting up a nursery in New Jersey in early 1786 where he grew many American trees and shrubs. In his first year, Michaux sent some 5000 young trees and several thousand packets of seeds to Versailles, traveling at the same time to Mount Vernon to deliver to

George Washington a gift of seeds of a cypress tree sent by Lafayette.

Conversations with the Bartrams drew his attention to the montane forests of the Carolinas, and in 1787, Michaux was finding many new species that had escaped the attention of John and William Bartram. With him was Michaux's son, François-André. So productive were their efforts that Michaux established a second nursery, this one in Charleston, South Carolina, and put Louis Bosc d'Antic in charge. In later years, Bosc became the French consul in South Carolina, and after he returned to Paris in 1800, a leading horticulturalist.

From Charleston, the Michauxs traveled to northern Florida in 1788 and on to the Bahamas in 1789. Awaiting a decision on his proposal to explore the West, the elder Michaux ventured into Canada going nearly to Hudson Bay in search of new species. On foot and by canoe, and led by Indian guides, Michaux collected all the dried specimens and seeds he and the others could carry.

Sending plants from America to Europe had never been routine. Many collectors lost their specimens to shipwrecks, floods, insects, or pirates. Michaux's 1786 collection was largely lost when a ship sank off the Dutch coast. Sea water, rain, and mold killed many seeds and young plants on their way across the Atlantic, and many a pack horse was lost while collecting in the field. The problems of field work were a never-ending challenge to the Michauxs, but little did André Michaux expect them to be compounded by international politics.

*Rose-bay* (Rhododendron maximum) *is the largest native American species of rhododendron. It was introduced early into Europe and is used in the development of many cultivated species.*

When Edmond Genét, the new French minister to the United States, arrived in the summer of 1793, he was prepared to lead his fellow citizens in Spanish Louisiana in revolt against Spain. With Jefferson's quiet approval and the volunteered help of George Rogers Clark, the major players were in position to invade from Kentucky. Jefferson's goal was the opening of the Mississippi River to navigation for the new United States. Citizen Genét's agent in Kentucky was André Michaux.

Jefferson was aware of Michaux's role, and the timing of the botanist's proposed expedition into upper Louisiana and on to the West Coast was understood to be a part of the plan of securing Louisiana (and if possible, Canada) for the French.

When Genét finally flagrantly violated American neutrality by involving the United States in France's war with Spain and Great Britain, and was removed from office in November of 1793, the original scheme collapsed. News of Genét's fate never reached Michaux, who arrived in Kentucky in September, having slowly collected his way from Washington to Lexington. Unaware that Jefferson had written and warned the governor about Michaux's political activities, the botanist continued to collect plants and play his small role in soliciting Americans to invade New Orleans. The botanical results were significant; those relating to an invasion force were not and thus Michaux remained free to roam the backwoods of America in search of new and interesting plants.

Jefferson still wanted Michaux to explore the West, and continued to

solicit funds for that purpose. When it became obvious that funding would not be forthcoming, Michaux sailed for France in 1796 knowing that his American nurseries were in good hands. He had the beginnings of a manuscript that would account for all of the known plants in North America, and this he was determined to publish forthwith.

The manuscript was reviewed by Antoine de Jussieu, the foremost promoter of a natural system, and by Louis Claude Richard, a professor of botany in Paris. Michaux labored intensely on his book, accepting many of the recommendations made by Richard. Illustrations for the work were prepared by Pierre Redouté, the Luxembourg-born botanical artist whose numerous volumes of flower paintings published a decade later would make him world-famous. François-André returned to the United States in 1800. In 1801, the elder Michaux sailed to Madagascar to collect, leaving the manuscript in limbo, and the younger Michaux concentrated on plants useful to understanding the flora of eastern North America. He remained until early 1803 when word arrived that his father was near death, and he was needed back in France to see the book into print. In March of 1803, *Flora boreali-americana* was published, followed shortly thereafter by the elder Michaux's death.

Jefferson's assumption of the presidency in 1800 only furthered his desire for a western expedition. It is said that if he had lost the election, he would have led the effort himself. What the nation gained by his election, science lost. From his new position, he could direct federal funds into such exploits, long supported by European governments, but as yet not sponsored by the United States.

The Treaty of San Ildefonso, which granted Louisiana to Napoleon, was signed in October of 1800 but kept secret. It was not until June of 1801 that Jefferson heard rumors that France was now America's western neighbor. France was a threat, and in early 1802 Jefferson asked Robert Livingston, the Minister to France, to make quiet inquiries on the future of Louisiana and Florida. In November, the Spanish still in control of New Orleans, closed the Mississippi River to American commerce, so that when Congress convened in December of 1802 it was a major political problem. In January, Jefferson asked for Congressional approval to allow James Monroe to negotiate rights to the Mississippi River and all the territories to the east. In secret, the House of Representatives allocated $2,000,000 to defray any expenses.

Monroe sailed for France in March of 1802 and began negotiations that lasted until late April of 1803 when, remarkably, Napoleon offered the United States the whole of the Louisiana Territory for $15,000,000. Napoleon ratified the treaty of cession in late May and on 14 July, 1803, the treaty reached Jefferson. As a strict believer in the Constitution, Jefferson was uncertain how to proceed. In mid-August, Jefferson was warned by

Livingston that Napoleon might change his mind and an extra session of Congress was held on October 17 to accept or reject the treaty. Soon, the treaty was ratified, and the size of the United States more than doubled.

Jefferson now had a valid excuse for the expedition to the Pacific Ocean that was already in the field.

In January of 1803, Jefferson sent a secret message to Congress request-

*Ribes sanguineum (far left) was collected by Lewis in 1806. It is one of the most beautiful ornamental shrubs native to the Pacific Northwest. The plant figured here is the var.* glutinosum, *found by Douglas in California.*

*Shallon* (Gaultheria shallon) *(left) was first collected by Menzies but named by Pursh who studied a Lewis specimen.*

ing $2500 for an overland expedition. Jefferson was trying to ease Native Americans from their homelands east of the Mississippi River either by incorporating them as second-class citizens into the United States or by aiding their departure for lands farther west. The expedition was to have commercial and military objectives, including the location of the best farmland for American settlement. As far as the public was concerned, however, the expedition's only object was to be scientific.

Jefferson selected his private secretary, Meriwether Lewis, to head the expedition, and Lewis invited his boyhood friend, William Clark, to be his co-leader. Neither was trained in the sciences.

Jefferson instructed his secretary to spend several weeks during the spring of 1803 in Philadelphia studying natural history with Benjamin Smith Barton. Lewis was a keen observer and rapidly learned the art of preparing plant and animal specimens. The expedition set out for the West on July 5, 1803, before word of the treaty reached the President. Winter quarters were established near St. Louis, and Lewis and Clark drilled their forty-eight men. On May 21, 1804, after watching the formal transfer of the Louisiana Territory from the Spanish to the French and from the French to the Americans, the Lewis and Clark expedition started up the

Missouri River in a keelboat and two pirogues. At La Charette, the last European settlement along the river, Lewis and Clark found Daniel Boone at his home and asked if he would like to join their party; the sixty-nine-year-old frontiersman declined at his wife's request. They overwintered on the east bank of the Missouri River just below the Knife River where a blockhouse was built and named Fort Mandan in honor of the neighboring Mandan Indians.

Lewis had been collecting plants along the Missouri River as the expedition moved upstream. In April of 1805, the specimens were sent down the Missouri River to Captain Amos Stoddard, the commandant in St. Louis; he sent them on to the President's home, Monticello, in Virginia. A total of sixty-seven plant specimens were among the boxes of animal skins, rock samples, and Native American artifacts. Jefferson went through the collection, sending the plants on to Barton who, in November, accessioned them into the *Donation Book* of the American Philosophical Society. Most of the remaining material went to Charles Willson Peale's Museum in Philadelphia.

The day the specimens headed for St. Louis on the keelboat, Lewis and Clark with thirty-one others headed west with the two pirogues and six canoes. Their guide was the famed French fur trapper, Toussaint Charbonneau, and his Shoshone wife, Sacajawea, who was carrying her recently born son on her back. By late June they were at the Great Falls in Montana. They spent eleven days in a portage around the falls and a month later were at the Three Forks of the Missouri River, which Lewis named for Thomas Jefferson, James Madison, and Albert Gallatin.

To this point, Clark was in charge of the transportation, with Lewis walking the banks of the river with his big Newfoundland dog, collecting whatever might catch his fancy. They followed the Jefferson fork, with Lewis traveling ahead in hopes of finding the Shoshone who might provide horses. He found a party and returned to Clark. To their surprise, Sacajawea, who had been captured by rival Indians in 1800 and sold to Charbonneau, recognized her brother, and horses and guides were assured.

*W*hile at the Great Falls of the Missouri, Lewis made two caches of specimens gathered since Fort Mandan. Unfortunately, the river flooded during the spring of 1806 and all the plants were lost. Other specimens were collected, and other caches made, including one along the Clearwater River in Idaho in October when the expedition started down the river. A month later, on November 7, 1805, Lewis saw the Pacific Ocean at the mouth of the Columbia River.

A dismal winter was spent in the cold and fog at Fort Clatsop, an outpost named for the local Indian people. In late March of 1806, the party started for home. Travel up the Columbia River was difficult, made all the more so by a lack of food. Still, Lewis collected specimens of plants, birds, fish, and mammals whenever he could. On the Camas Plains of Idaho, Lewis found Camas lily, *Camassia quamash*, whose bulb was used by the Shoshone for food, and as he labored up the Lolo Pass in the Bitterroot

Pl. 1.<sup></sup>

JUGLANS nigra
*Black Walnut*

Pl. 36.

QUERCUS rubra
*Red Oak*

Pl. 7.

JUGLANS squamosa
*Shell bark Hickory*

Pl. 6.

BIGNONIA Catalpa
*Catalpa*

Mountains, he gathered the plant that would afterward bear his name, *Lewisia rediviva*. Once east of the Continental Divide, the homeward trip was rapid. They reached the Mandan villages on August 14, and were in St. Louis on September 23, 1806.

Lewis took his seeds and plant specimens to Barton. Lewis was arranging his journals, and wished to have the scientific names for the plants when he published. Barton, who was displeased with Michaux's flora, was attempting to write his own book. To assist him, he employed a Saxon-born botanist named Frederick Pursh. When Pursh arrived in Philadelphia, he was the gardener at Woodlands, the estate of William Hamilton. The seeds were sent to Woodlands by Barton, and with them went the dried plant specimens. In late 1806, Barton employed Pursh, but the two men were soon at odds, and Pursh left Philadelphia for the Elgin Botanic Garden in New York.

The New York garden was started in 1801 by David Hosack on ground now occupied by Rockefeller Center. The garden was large and well-stocked with a diversity of European and American species. When Pursh left Philadelphia, he took with him seeds and cuttings of several of the Lewis plants, including the Osage orange, a botanical marvel Lewis had seen in cultivation in St. Louis and collected on both legs of his travels on the Missouri River. By 1811, Pursh was at odds with Hosack, and complaining that he found America "very unfavourable to the publication of scientific works," he left for England.

How Pursh came to have some of the Lewis collection in his possession is unknown. According to Pursh, Lewis gave him the specimens. This seems unlikely as they clearly were meant for Barton. There is no question that Barton charged Pursh with the task of reviewing the specimens at the Philosophical Society, or that Pursh was to describe and illustrate the specimens Lewis gave to Barton in the fall of 1806. Equally certain was Barton's assumption that Pursh would turn over the information to his employer. How Pursh came to still have the specimens in 1811 when he left the United States is a mystery.

In London, Pursh showed his manuscript on the plants of America to Aylmer Lambert, a gentlemen of leisure interested in botany who was in the process of assembling a large herbarium and library. He provided Pursh with a room, beer, paper and specimens, and got him to finish the manuscript. In late December of 1813, Pursh's *Flora americae septentrionalis* was published.

This episode was not the only reason why Pursh would later be characterized as one of the most unscrupulous of the early botanists. He also attempted to describe new American species found by others.

In 1808, at the age of 22, the English naturalist Thomas Nuttall arrived in Philadelphia where his enthusiasm for botany and exploration quickly brought him to the attention of Benjamin Smith Barton, who was spending most of the summer at the home of John and William Bartram on the banks of the Schuylkill.

Nuttall realized that while men like the Bartrams and Barton were knowledgeable, the likelihood that a major botanical work on North

American plants would come from them was nil; the Bartrams because of age and duties, Barton because of a lack of ability. And the locally written works that were available were rapidly becoming out of date. Thomas Walter's *Flora caroliniana* published in 1788 was more complete than Gronovius's second edition of *Flora virginica*, but neither made any attempt to account for the plants to the north. Humphry Marshall, the cousin of the younger John Bartram, had a large arboretum at Marshallton, his home in Chester County, Pennsylvania. He accounted for many of its species in a 1785 catalog entitled *Arbustrum americanum*. Gotthilf Heinrich Muhlenberg, the son of Heinrich Melchior Muhlenberg who championed Lutheranism in North America, was a Philadelphia native educated in Halle, Germany. His earliest botanical paper, "Index flora lancastriensis," was published in the *Transactions of the American Philosophical Society* in 1791. In this work he accounted for 454 genera and more than a thousand native and cultivated species that grew in the vicinity of his home in Lancaster.

In Virginia, Dr. James Greenway attempted to write a new flora of Virginia, accounting for the species discovered by John Banister in the late 1600s and by Catesby in the 1710s, but never completed the task. The Charleston physician, John Linnaeus Shecut, published *Flora carolinaeensis* in 1806, but only the first volume made it into print, and while detailed, it accounted for only the native and cultivated plants in the Carolinas.

The younger Michaux returned to Paris in late 1807 and was preparing his *Histoire des arbres forestiers de l'Amérique septentrionale* for the publisher. The three volumes were published from 1810 until 1813, and illustrated with 140 stipple-engraved, color-printed (and retouched by hand) illustrations, most of them drawn by members of the Redouté family.

Nuttall also met John Lyon, the Scottish gardener who replaced Pursh at Woodlands in 1806, and the nurseryman Bernard M'Mahon who sold seeds and botany books in Philadelphia. M'Mahon's *American gardeners' calendar*, first published in 1806, eventually went through eleven editions over the next 50 years. It was Jefferson who recommended to Lewis that some of the Louisiana seeds go to M'Mahon, and it was M'Mahon who was to oversee Pursh when he examined, for Barton, Lewis's dried specimens. Another of Nuttall's early contacts was Zaccheus Collins, a Quaker merchant and philanthropist who encouraged Nuttall to collect minerals as well as plants.

Barton's 1803 textbook, *Elements of botany*, was soon in Nuttall's hands as were the specimens in his herbarium and the books in his library. He also saw some of the early volumes of Carl Ludwig Willdenow's revision of Linnaeus's *Species plantarum* in which several new American species were described from specimens Muhlenberg sent to Willdenow. Nuttall also

found journal articles written by the Constantinople-born Samuel Constantine Rafinesque-Schmalz in an American journal, *New York Medical Repository*, published by Dr. Samuel Latham Mitchill. Rafinesque was highly critical of Michaux's *Flora* and vowed to write a new work, although at the time he was in Sicily.

*I*n early June of 1809, Nuttall left Philadelphia on his first field trip sponsored by Barton. He visited the salt marshes of Delaware Bay, sending Barton forty-three specimens gathered during the week-long trip. From there, Nuttall sailed south to the Nanticoke River on the Chesapeake Bay, returning at the end of the month with more material. Barton was pleased, and asked Nuttall to take a second trip, this time to the north and west to New York and the grand cataract of Niagara, following the general route on which Barton had sent Pursh in 1807. Leaving in early August, he gathered several hundred specimens of plants and minerals, including several fossils, as he made his way toward Lake Ontario. Illness overtook him in the fall, and he was unable to care for the living material. He lost all of his plants; even his dried collection was eaten up by mold. He returned to Philadelphia, dejected, and worked as a typesetter for a local printer to earn enough money to return to the field the following year.

While Barton was disappointed with Nuttall's efforts, he was more depressed to learn in January of 1810 that Meriwether Lewis was dead. Jefferson had appointed Lewis military governor of the Louisiana Territory in 1808, and his former secretary was torn between his new responsibilities and those of completing his report on his expedition. On the way to see Jefferson in October, 1809, Lewis died in an inn on the Natchez Trace near Nashville, Tennessee. Whether he was murdered or committed suicide was never resolved. It was George Rogers Clark who brought the news to Barton, along with a request for aid. With the help of Nicholas Biddle and Paul Allen, *History of the expedition* was finally published in 1814 at a financial loss to all involved.

Clark asked Barton to write an account of the plants and animals, and to list all of the Indian words learned by Lewis. It is not known if Barton ever informed Clark that he no longer had the specimens, for his reports to the explorer were always positive. In any event, there is no evidence Barton did anything to accomplish the tasks asked of him.

If there was another motive in Barton asking Nuttall to collect for him in the Old Northwest it might have been in hopes that Nuttall would somehow rediscover many of the plants found further to the west by Lewis and Clark. Barton also built a greenhouse and established a garden to grow western plants. As always, Barton's plans were ambitious.

Barton drew up a contract that paid Nuttall eight dollars a month and all his field expenses in exchange for the rights to all of Nuttall's specimens. He also required Nuttall not to communicate any findings without his prior approval. In early April, 1810, Nuttall left Philadelphia for Pittsburgh. His companion, for much of the trip, was the Spanish fur trader, Manuel Lisa of St. Louis. Lisa filled Nuttall with tales of the West and the diversity of plants that could be found. Nuttall was intrigued, but his travels led him

*The salmon berry (Rubus spectabilis) was found by Lewis along the Columbia River and is now occasionally found in the garden. The beauty of its showy flowers and fruits belies its aggressive nature when it escapes from cultivation.*

to the north, not the west, and the two men parted at Pittsburgh.

Nuttall collected his way to the southern shore of Lake Erie which he followed past Cleveland to the mouth of the Huron River. Here he joined a group of surveyors and by canoe, and with many stops, crossed through Lake Huron and Lake Michigan to the mouth of the Fox River. At each landfall, as camp was being prepared, Nuttall was off collecting.

This was not what Barton had suggested, as Nuttall was to have gone overland to Chicago, and then on to Canada. Such travel by a lone naturalist who had to transport all of his equipment as well as specimens was simply impossible. At least in a large canoe manned by French-Canadian voyagers Nuttall was able to move rapidly through the region and collect at many different locations. By mid-August, Nuttall was on Lake Superior at Mackinac Island, the headquarters of John Jacob Astor's American Fur Company, and a place filled with music and taverns.

Nuttall learned that the British controlled access to Lake Superior and there was no way that he could proceed into Canada. But an alternative was suddenly placed before him in the form of Wilson Price Hunt, the overland leader of a group called Astor's Pacific Fur Company. If he wished, Nuttall could go with them and follow Lewis and Clark's route to the Pacific.

The exploits of this trip would be recorded by Washington Irving in an American classic, *Astoria*. Nuttall's diary was not rediscovered and published until 1951, and despite many factual errors in Irving's account that came to light, *Astoria* still records the thrills and difficulties of western exploration. By the end of August, the party was on the Fox River, and in early September were at the portage over to the Wisconsin River. Nuttall was in a botanical heaven, finding many new species in the Wisconsin

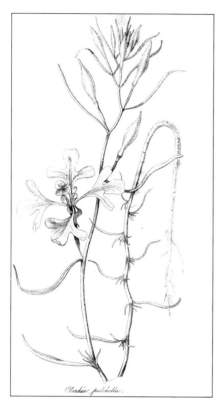

*Frederick Pursh established the genus* Clarkia *to honor William Clark, publishing this plate of* Clarkia pulchella *in his 1813 book* Flora americae septentrionalis.

prairies. By the time Nuttall reached St. Louis three weeks later, he had collections of some 220 different species.

He did not expect to hear of another collector in the city of 1400 on the banks of the Mississippi.

In August of 1809, John Bradbury, on a collecting trip for the Liverpool Botanic Garden, arrived at Monticello and for more than two weeks discussed horticulture and botanical explorations with Jefferson. The former President recommended that he explore the country west of the Mississippi, as Jefferson was convinced that this area would be rich in new species of value to gardeners. Bradbury worked his way westward, arriving in St. Louis on the last day of the year. He established a small nursery to overwinter his living material, and spent the growing season of 1810 collecting along the Mississippi River. Bradbury often traveled with Henry Marie Brackenridge, the son of Judge Hugh Brackenridge of Pittsburgh and author of *Modern chivalry*, a novel describing life on the American frontier. In St. Louis, young Henry, a lawyer by training, spent most of his time writing articles for the *Missouri Gazette*.

Initially Nuttall and Bradbury had little time to talk science. Nuttall was probably working as a typesetter for Joseph Charless, the publisher of the *Missouri Gazette*, while Bradbury was preparing to send a large collection of dried and living specimens to Europe. Nuttall and Bradbury visited mines south of St. Louis, and no doubt talked about the plants they saw. Nuttall, in particular, collected seeds, including those of Missouri evening primrose, *Oenothera macrocarpa*. Near the city, Nuttall collected many new species that he would later name, and in gardens he saw the Osage orange. In 1818, he proposed the name *Maclura aurantiaca* for this plant, although Rafinesque had proposed *Toxylon pomiferum* for the same plant a year earlier. Today, this strange tree, for technical reasons, is known as *Maclura pomifera*, a joining of both Nuttall's and Rafinesque's names.

Price's Overland Astorians, as they would be known, left St. Louis in March of 1811 without either botanist, who were both waiting for the mail to arrive the following day. When Bradbury sent his 1810 collection to his patron William Roscoe, he said he would collect along the Arkansas River in 1811. He did not mention that he had already agreed to accompany Price and his Pacific Fur Company up the Missouri River. Nuttall was no more open with Barton, and didn't divulge his whereabouts. Such details were soon forgotten as both men were with Price, collecting along the shore as the fur company worked their boats up the River.

At La Charette, Bradbury talked with Daniel Boone. The following day he talked with John Colter who had discovered "Colter's Hell," better known today as Yellowstone, during the winter of 1807-1808 while trapping for Manual Lisa. Colter told Price of the dangers he faced from the Blackfoot and argued for a more southern route through the Wind River Range, but the band continued up the Missouri.

*Bear grass* (Xerophyllum tenax) *was found by Lewis as he ascended Lolo Pass. The fragment collected by him was illllustrated by William Hooker for Pursh's* Flora.

Dried plants, rocks, minerals, fossils, and animal skins of no worldly value except to the naturalists were soon adding their weight to the boats being pulled up the Missouri. The new species were everywhere. Both men gathered the common buffalo grass, *Buchlë dactyloides*, the scarlet false mallow, *Sphaeralcea coccinea*, and the gumbo evening primrose, *Oenothera caespitosa*. The further up the River, and the later in the growing season, the more new species they found .

Travel on the Missouri was not without its problems. Indian wars were common, and when the Astorians were suddenly confronted with some 600 Yankton and Teton Sioux, guns were quickly placed at the ready. For Nuttall, this was a problem. He used the barrel of his rifle to dig out plants and, when plugged, to hold seeds.

Some 1200 miles from St. Louis, the Overland Astorians were overtaken by Manuel Lisa and members of his Missouri Fur Company. With Lisa were Charbonneau and Sacajawea as well as Henry Brackenridge. It was not surprising that the two fur companies were hostile. A battle

*The cranberry (*Vaccinium macrocarpon) *was illustrated by William Paul Crillon Barton for* A flora of North America *published in 1820 and 1821. All of his illustrations were drawn from live plants observed in the wild.*

between them was halted by Bradbury and Brackenridge, who soothed hard feelings.

At an Arikaras village, Hunt decided to purchase horses and ride westward, leaving the Missouri to Lisa. The naturalists joined Lisa and continued up river, with Bradbury riding ahead to Fort Mandan with some of Lisa's men to secure horses. On this portion of the trip, Bradbury found several new species not seen by Nuttall, who remained on the river.

Fort Mandan had been relocated from the site selected by Lewis and Clark, and was now manned by Reuben Lewis, Meriwether's only brother. Into Lewis's garden, Nuttall and Bradbury were soon transplanting living plants, and scouting the nearby hills for curious plants. In early July, Bradbury and Breckinridge returned to St. Louis; Nuttall remained at Fort Mandan until autumn. It is thought that Nuttall walked at least 200 miles further upstream to collect a sago lily later named for him, *Calochortus nuttallii*; an elegant pincushion cactus, *Mammillaria vivipara*; and the Great Plains soapweed, *Yucca glauca*.

Nuttall returned to St. Louis in late October, 1811. His return was much easier than Bradbury's had been. Ten days after reaching the city,

Bradbury was ill, and in August submitted a letter of resignation to Roscoe. It was not until December that he was able to travel, and was on the Mississippi River when the great New Madrid earthquake hit on the early morning of December 16. His boat rode out the churning water, and managed to avoid the downed trees, floating fragments of broken boats, and floating islands. He reached New Orleans in mid-January of 1812. Nuttall left St. Louis shortly after Bradbury arrived. Nuttall made an occasional collection along the river and around New Orleans; from there he sailed to England in December.

To fulfill his contract with Barton, Nuttall sent to Philadelphia dried specimens, seeds, and his notes. Barton was pleased with the collections, but it was Nuttall he wanted more. He had hoped that once Nuttall had returned from the West he would write the long-awaited manuscript on the Lewis and Clark collection.

When Bradbury arrived in New Orleans, he shipped his herbarium specimens to his son, John, and sailed for New York. He was still in America when the War of 1812 began, and he was trapped for the duration of the war. His son, upon receipt of the specimens, and without clear instructions to the contrary, handed them over to William Roscoe. That proved, for Bradbury, to be the final blow of bad luck.

Fraser's Nursery at Sloane Square in London had long sold American plants. John Fraser saw Walter's *Flora* into print, and was then in possession of Walter's hortus siccus of dried Carolina plants. The younger John Fraser and his brother James continued the business after their father died in 1811, and they were eager to sell Nuttall's plants. To promote the new seeds, the Frasers asked Nuttall to write a catalog describing and naming the many species, highlighting the new species. A total of eighty-nine species were mentioned, of which seventeen were validly described as new to science. A catalog of new and interesting plants collected in Upper Louisiana was published in the spring of 1813. Many of the most elegant garden species were published in *Curtis's botanical magazine* by a variety of people, but only one was proposed by Nuttall himself as he still regarded himself obliged to Barton.

Frederick Pursh felt no such obligation. When Nuttall proudly showed him a new blazing star, Pursh asked Nuttall for a description and proceeded to publish it in *Curtis's botanical magazine*. To add insult, the accompanying plate was drawn from Nuttall's garden material. Bradbury's specimens were soon in Pursh's hands. William Bullock bought the specimens from Bradbury's son at Roscoe's request, and then proceeded to deliver them to Sir Joseph Banks whose botanical fame came from this trip on the *Endeavour* to Australia and his support of the voyages of Captain James Cook. Banks, unable to name the specimens himself, sent them on to Lambert, and Lambert gave them to Pursh.

Suddenly Pursh had access to the Louisiana specimens Nuttall had been unwilling to share, and he incorporated the new species into his manuscript on the plants of temperate North America.

*This finger poppy-mallow (Callirhoe digitata) was found by Nuttall on his Arkansas expedition of 1819. William Barton proposed* Nuttallia *for this plant in August 1822, after Nuttall proposed* Callirhoe *for the same plant in 1821.*

*E*ver since Pursh had returned to England he had been attending meetings of the Linnean Society of London. In January of 1812, the first part of a manuscript on the plants discovered by Lewis and Clark was read, with subsequent parts following over the next several months. Pursh rushed new genera into print, notably *Lewisia, Clarkia,* and *Calochortus.* In February, 1813, Pursh described *Hosackia,* naming the plant for his last American employer, David Hosack. At the same time, Pursh was visiting herbaria at the British Museum and the University of Oxford where he examined specimens collected by Banister, Catesby, and the Bartrams. Just before Christmas of 1813, Pursh presented the Linnean Society with a copy of his *Flora americae septentrionalis.*

The two-volume work was a vast improvement over that published by Michaux a decade before. The descriptions were more detailed, the distribution data more complete, and the number of species greatly increased. Nuttall was distresssed to see names for many of his new species, and Jefferson, who had wanted Lewis and Clark's new species to be described in Lewis's journal, was equally disappointed.

It would not be until 1819 that Congress would authorize another western expedition, and by then, much of the botanical wealth of the American West was being examined by botanists in Paris, London, and St. Petersburg.

# VI

# *In Search of Magnificent Trees*

*Douglas fir* (Pseudotsuga menziesii).

For temperate Europe, elegant park-like estates with exotic trees were the ultimate sign of position, wealth, and stature. Trees were featured prominently in most garden designs, and the abundant diversity of flowering trees in eastern North America made botanical expeditions to this part of the New World particularly rewarding. With the opening of botanical explorations in China in 1700, however, interest shifted from what is now the eastern United States to southeastern China and Japan. The floras of southern North America and Asia have an usually large number of genera in common. To eager nurserymen, the thought of having for sale new species of already proven genera was more than they could have hoped for. Suddenly, the interest of botanical exploration shifted from the New World to the farthest edge of the Old.

By the mid 1700s, explorers in North America were concentrating on the lesser plants: algae, fungi, lichens, mosses, and the herbaceous flowering plants. There were many new species to find, and with the ever-expanding interest in annual flowering borders for formal gardens, more and more American plants were introduced to satisfy the new fashion. When the sailing ships of the French, English, and Russians began to ply the West Coast of North America, naturalists found plenty of flowering shrubs and trees to immediately satisfy their sponsors, but more astounding were the giant conifers that so dominated the landscape—pines, firs, larches, and redwoods. Estate holders quickly realized the trees' commercial value if they could be successfully grown in northern Europe. Once it was found they could be, the rush was on to bring them to Europe. Foremost in the hunt was David Douglas of the Royal Horticultural Society who first went to the Oregon Country in 1825.

Douglas was not the first naturalist to see the magnificent trees along

*The lupines were a favorite group of David Douglas and he ascribed names to many different species. He found* Lupinus lepidus *near the Great Falls of the Columbia River in 1825.*

the Oregon coast, many of which would eventually bear his name, nor was he the first to collect and name them.

Long before Douglas went to Oregon, Spanish galleons plied the Pacific Coast of North America, sailing from Mexico to the Philippines carrying gold, spices, silk, and chinaware. In 1578, Sir Francis Drake, an Elizabethan Sea Hawk, and his crew on the *Golden Hind*, raided Spanish treasure galleons from Peru to Mexico, and claimed California for England in 1579. As long as there was gold to find or take, interest in wild flowers and trees was nonexistent. The defeat of the Spanish Armada in 1588 did much to curtail Spain's wealth and energy, but even when the Spanish once again sailed the Pacific in the late 1590s and early 1600s, no attention was given to the natural resources of Mexico and California. Sebastián Vizcaíno enthusiastically reported on the harbors at San Diego, Monterey, and Drake's Bay in 1602, and called for settlements to frustrate the English, but little was said of the vegetation except that it was bountiful. Even as the Spanish moved northward into the greater Southwest of Texas, New Mexico, and California over the next two centuries, essentially no attention was paid to the plant life.

That changed with the arrival, in 1791, of Alessandro Malaspina, for aboard his corvettes he carried naturalists and artists on a five-year, round-the-world expedition. The two naturalists were Thaddaeus Haenke and Luis Née. Née remained in Acapulco while Malaspina, with Haenke, sailed north to Nootka Sound, near what is now known as Vancouver Island. Haenke botanized whenever possible from Alaska southward, and extensively around Monterey in September, gathering both dried specimens and seeds.

The journals of the Malaspina expedition were not published until 1885, in large part because, upon his returned to Spain in 1795, Malaspina was imprisoned. He was freed in 1802, only to die in 1809 having never recovered from his confinement. Née described the California live oak, *Quercus agrifolia*, and the California white oak, *Quercus lobata*, in 1801, but the vast majority of Haenke's new species were not published for years. From 1825 until 1835, the Czech botanist and curator of the Prague National Museum, Carl Presl, published *Reliquiae haenkeanae* in seven parts arranged in two volumes. While this work accounted for all of Haenke's specimens, by then only a few from California were new to science. One still undescribed species was California fuchsia, *Zauschneria californica*, described in 1835.

Née returned to Spain with some 10,000 specimens, drawings, and numerous seeds, including some from California given him by Haenke. The seeds were planted at the botanical garden in Madrid, and several hundred species were described by Antonio José Cavanilles and Mariano Lagasca y Segura. Only a few from California were mentioned.

Interestingly, the Russians were the first to make important botanical discoveries in western North America. In 1741, Georg Steller, a German physician with the Vitus Bering expedition that crossed Siberia, reached Kodiak Island off the coast of Alaska where he collected 141 species of plants in six hours. His huge collection of plant and animal specimens was taken back to Kamchatka where, in the winter of 1741-1742, Bering and most of the company died. The survivors made their way to Petropavlovsk where Steller remained until 1744, sending, on rare occasions, a few of his specimens back to St. Petersburg. His own return across Siberia ended in death in 1746, and only a portion of his collection made it back to civilization. None of his Alaskan plants was saved. Nonetheless, what little made its way to Linnaeus was impressive. In 1753, Linnaeus accounted for several of the new species *Steller* found on Kamchatka, and in 1759, Linnaeus described many new species of animals, including the blue fox, the Pacific walrus and the noisy Steller jay.

*E*ven the first plant to be described from California was the result of a French, not a Spanish, expedition. In 1786, a French expedition under the command of Jean-François de Galaup, Comte de Lapérouse, entered Monterey Bay. Aboard the two frigates was a scientific staff of ten, including a gardener named Jean-Nicolas Collignon. They had left France in 1785 and sailed around the Horn to Chile, then the Hawaiian Islands, and on into Alaska to about sixty degrees north latitude. In September of the following year they visited Monterey Bay where Collignon gave the Spanish governor and the mission fathers seeds he had brought from Paris and potatoes he had gathered in Chile.

After ten days, the expedition sailed for China and on to Australia. At Botany Bay, in February of 1788, Lapérouse sent many of his records and some of the scientific collections to France, including seeds gathered at Monterey. It was not for another forty years that the fate of the expedition was known, when remains of one of the ships were found in the Solomon Islands. The Monterey seeds were grown at the Jardin des Plantes in Paris, and in 1789, Antoine Laurent de Jussieu established the genus *Abronia* for the plant in his *Genera plantarum*, and in 1791, Jean Baptise de Lamarck named the species *Abronia umbellata*, the scientific name of the beach sand verbena.

David Douglas had plenty of time to think about the botanical treasures that were to be found around Fort Vancouver located upstream from the mouth of the Columbia River. The Hudson's Bay Company ship *William and Ann* reached the Columbia on February 10, 1825, nearly six months out of Gravesend. It would be another six weeks before the weather calmed, the ship could enter the river, and Douglas could collect his first plant. It was a far different reception for Archibald Menzies when he sailed along the coast in 1792.

Menzies first came to North America in 1785 as ship's surgeon aboard *HMS Assistance* on the Halifax station off the coast of Canada. He collected specimens for Sir Joseph Banks, visiting many of the same islands Banks had been on in 1766. No sooner had Menzies returned to England than he boarded the merchant ship *Prince of Wales* bound for the cold waters of Alaska and the fur trade. He visited Nootka Sound in July of 1787 and collected several new species, including *Menziesia ferruginea*, an ornamental shrub. Most were not named until much later, and by then

many had been found by others.

Menzies efforts were fully appreciated by Banks, and when plans were being formulated for a voyage around the world under the command of George Vancouver, Banks secured the position of surgeon-naturalist for Menzies aboard the flagship, the *Discovery*.

Vancouver's charge was to map the Pacific Coast of North America from San Francisco to present-day British Columbia. Like all other explorers of his day, he was also charged to search for the Northwest Passage, that long-sought ice-free route north of Canada from the Atlantic to the Pacific. He was an experienced but severe ship's captain who had served with James Cook on the latter's second and third voyages. He was tolerant but not always supportive of naturalists' needs to go ashore or to protect their collections from the ravages of the sea.

*Mr. Drummond's rudbeckia,
(Rudbeckia drummondii)
from Paxton's Magazine of
Botany, Vol. VI.*

*B*anks was concerned that in spite of the Admiralty's approval of his detailed instructions to Menzies, Vancouver would make collecting difficult for the naturalist. Even Lord William Grenville, leader of the House of Lords, directly instructed the Admiralty to impress upon the commander "that he was to afford every degree of assistance to Mr. Menzies." Their concern was prescient.

The *Discovery*, with the brig *Chatham* and the store ship *Doedalus*, left England on April 1, 1791, and went around the Cape of Good Hope to Australia. After brief stops in Tahiti and the Hawaiian Islands, the ships arrived off the coast of northern California a year later. Vancouver sailed northward and by the end of the month entered the Straits of Juan de Fuca. There they encountered Captain Robert Gray and his ship the *Columbia*, the first American ship to sail round the world and the namesake of the Columbia River, which Gray would discover a few weeks later.

Menzies's first landing was at Port Discovery, a narrow bay southwest of Port Townsend, Jefferson County, Washington. From the first moment he was on shore, Menzies found species of plants never before seen by naturalists, many that would later carry his name. One of his first was madrona, *Arbutus menziesii*, named by Pursh in 1813.

The pattern was set. Vancouver moved his small fleet about what became Vancouver Island, occasionally allowing Menzies to go ashore and collect. To ensure more specimens than he himself might collect, Menzies encouraged others to collect whatever they might be allowed to bring aboard ship.

Menzies found several giant forest trees on Vancouver Island. One was nearly 300 feet tall, the same tree that later caught Douglas's attention as he entered the Columbia River. The coastal forest was dominated by the species now scientifically known as *Pseudotsuga menziesii* and commonly called Douglas fir. It is the most important lumber tree in the Pacific Northwest. At Nootka, Menzies found another tall tree, *Thuja plicata*, the arborvitae. Seeds of both were collected and taken to England where the trees have flourished ever since.

While at Nootka, Menzies visited with José Mariano Moçiño, one of the naturalists aboard the *Aranzaza* with the Malaspina expedition. With the Spaniard was the artist Athanasio Echeverría. Moçiño probably collected plants during his travels along the Pacific Coast in 1791, but if so, none of the specimens exist today. Echeverría made about 200 elegant drawings of plants in the Nootka area. Both men are best known for their botanical discoveries in Mexico, but like so much of Spain's early botanical efforts, their discoveries went unpublished. Moçiño's journal was not published until 1913, and an account of his botanical finds made with Martin de Sessé y Lacasta went unpublished until 1887, decades after their significance was of any scientific importance.

Each winter, Vancouver and his men sailed to the Hawaiian Islands, and there Menzies collected. After spending the summer months of 1792 again sailing near Vancouver Island, the expedition turned southward along the Pacific Coast, reaching San Francisco Bay in mid-October. Although the season was late, Menzies gathered seeds of several species, but dried only a few specimens. From early November until mid-January of 1793, the expedition was anchored at Monterey Bay. Once again the season was late, the conditions dry, and a prolonged illness reduced Menzies's opportunities to collect. Nonetheless, several new species were found.

With the increased sea traffic along the Pacific Coast, Menzies was able to send boxes of specimens back to England almost once a year, along with letters and reports. One such shipment left California in January of 1793 on the *Activa* bound for London; a day later, Vancouver and his men sailed for Hawaii, but instead of returning to the northern waters Vancouver returned to California in May. Some of the crew went ashore for water at Trinidad Head, and one returned with a flowering gooseberry that Pursh named *Ribes menziesii*; three weeks later they were once again at Nootka Sound.

In October, with Menzies aboard the *Chatham* under the command of Lieutenant Puget, the men explored the area north of San Francisco Bay. Puget was more willing to allow Menzies ashore to explore for plants, but few were gathered because much of the headlands had burned in recent fires. In San Francisco, it was not fires but the Spanish who now restricted Menzies' activities. Similar restrictions were imposed in Monterey, but not in Santa Barbara or San Diego. For two weeks, Menzies was allowed to collect, and he roamed the mountains behind the mission in Santa Barbara and its nearby marshes. In San Diego, Vancouver once again forbade Menzies from going ashore, and in sympathy, officers and crewmen alike brought him specimens. Even the mission fathers sent plants to Menzies, including seeds of the jojoba. It would be another forty years before this shrub and its prized oily seeds would be gathered again.

After another winter in Hawaii, Menzies was back along the northern coast, and now familiar with the more common species, he was searching for the strange and curious. In October of 1794, Vancouver sailed directly from Nootka Sound to Monterey Bay, arriving in early November. This time, both the Spanish and the ship's commander allowed Menzies to go ashore, and the reward was magnificent. On a three-day trip to the mission at Santa Cruz, specimens of a huge tree were collected; it was

*Menzies' platycarpos* (Lupinus densiflorus var. menziesii) *(above) was found by Archibald Menzies in the 1790s but not named until 1835. It was introduced into cultivation by William Lobb in 1853.*
Ponderosa pine (Pinus ponderosa) *(right).*

the coastal redwood, *Sequoia sempervirens*. Haenke found the tree and gathered specimens in 1791, but it was Menzies's specimens that were used to describe the species and announce it to the world. Amazingly, its name was not proposed until 1823 when Aylmer Lambert considered it a new species of *Taxodium*, related to the bald cypress of eastern North America. It was not until 1847 that Stephen Endlicher established *Sequoia* for the California tree.

On December 2, 1794, Vancouver began his long voyage home. Menzies had obtained more than three hundred species, the vast majority new to science. Upon arriving in England, he dutifully delivered all of his collections, notes, and journals to Sir Joseph Banks. No one took responsibility for their identification, but the first set of specimens went to the British Museum, with additional sets going to other botanists elsewhere in Europe. James Edward Smith, the President of the Linnean Society of London, received a large set, and described several species in Abraham Rees's *Cyclopaedia*. Pursh saw Menzies's specimens in the herbaria of the British Museum and Oxford. Lambert obtained a small set of mainly woody plants of potential horticultural importance, and those that Pursh did not described in 1813, he accounted for over the next three decades. Only now, in the 1990s, is the Menzies collection being reassembled and studied. While no new species await discovery, our understanding of the flora in the old-growth forests of the Pacific Northwest will be better understood.

*Mountain heather* (Phyllodoce empetriformis) *first collected by Menzies.*

On April 11, 1825, the *William and Ann* entered the Columbia River and for seven days the ship made its way up to Fort George, the former site of America's Fort Astoria, where David Douglas was met by John McLoughlin, the chief factor (field administrator of Hudson's Bay Company) at Fort Vancouver. Two days later Douglas was at the Hudson's Bay Company's newest post, some ninety miles from the Pacific. He immediately began to collect and gather seeds of the magnificent trees.

Douglas's charge from the Royal Horticultural Society was to collect seeds of the trees and flowering shrubs in particular, and such herbs as might be of potential value in the garden. He took his instruction seriously, and within days he was making short trips up and down the Columbia River, often traveling by canoe to the more interior posts. In August he and a party traveled up the Willamette River where he met with the Calapooie Indians, one of who told him of a giant tree far to the south with a huge cone. It was Douglas's first hint of sugar pine. When the *William and Ann* set sail for England in October, it carried sixteen large bundles of dried plants and a large chest of seeds. In addition, Douglas sent specimens of birds and animals as well as articles of Native American dress.

For all of his experience as a collector, Douglas was continually plagued with injury-causing accidents. In early October, Douglas fell driving a nail into his knee. For nearly three weeks he was restricted to Fort Vancouver, frustrated by his inability to collect seeds. With a still-infected knee, he set off to collect north of the Columbia to the coast north of Gray's Harbor, and was not back at the fort until mid-November. Much of the time he was on foot and traveling alone, made all the more miserable by the rain. It took him until mid-March, 1826, to recover from the trip and process his seeds and specimens. On the 19th he joined a party heading upriver bound for Kettle Falls.

The party reached The Dalles, just below the Falls of the Columbia River, on the evening of the 23rd where they were met by several Native Americans who came to receive gifts in payment for the trappers' safe passage up the river. By morning there were some 450, and they demanded more than twice the normal amount of tobacco. That evening, Alexander McLeod, the head of the party, learned that the Indians planned to pillage the boats, and with several of his men, including Douglas, he went to face the challenge. When McLeod pushed one of the young men, another pulled a handful of arrows from his quiver. Douglas immediately leveled his gun full of buckshot at the offender. One of the chiefs and three of his young men came forward and with a few words the incident was over. However, the fact that King George's Chief, the Grass Man, as Douglas was known, had drawn his rifle meant that an offense had been committed. A few days later, Douglas gave the six-foot, six-inch-tall chief a shilling he had carried in his pocket since leaving London, presenting it as a gift and the offense was forgiven.

*Two Douglas fir cones (Pseudotsuga menziesii).*

Except for Lewis and Clark, naturalists were generally restricted to the immediate coast. English explorers, under the leadership of Edward Parry and John Franklin searched for the Northwest Passage far to the north as Douglas traveled up the Columbia. John Richardson, author of *Fauna boreali-americana*, was with the Franklin expedition collecting animals while his assistant, Thomas Drummond, botanized far inland, eventually reaching the Canadian Rockies. When the boats were not under sail, Douglas walked the shore of the river. Even so, by April 11 the party was at the mouth of the Spokane River, and Kettle Falls was reached on the 22nd. Once again, the large trees caught Douglas's attention, and specimens of *Larix occidentalis*, the western larch, were gathered. He found one thirty feet in circumference.

While at Kettle Falls, Douglas broke the hammer on his rifle. With two horses and the two sons of Jacques Finlay he set off overland following the Coville River. At the abandoned post of Spokane House, Finlay repaired the rifle. On this trip, Douglas found ponderosa pine, *Pinus ponderosa*, a tall, straight tree able to reach more than 200 feet into the mountain air.

Back at Kettle Falls, Douglas continued to collect numerous new species of flowering herbs. Seeds were frustratingly few this early in the season, but the many specimens told of the great diversity. Flowering shrubs, most notably species of gooseberry, were particularly numerous, and Douglas found many that would prove to be wondrous additions to the English garden. Today, many of Douglas's new species may be seen in London's neighborhood parks.

Life in the field was not kind to Douglas. Illness, sore muscles, and swarmed, and meals were only occasionally warm. Mice ate his seeds, mold attacked his specimens, and at Fort Walla Walla rats carried off his razor and soap brush. In late August he lost the rest of his possessions when his canoe sank near Fort Okanagan; saving his specimens was more important than was rescuing even the rifle he had labored so hard to get repaired.

*The montane lady slipper (Cypripedium montanum), a rare species even in the days of David Douglas who proposed the name, is now an endangered and almost extinct species threatened by people who attempt to transplant the plant, not realizing that the effort will fail because of the unique relationship of the orchid to its companion fungal flora.*

Communication was always chancy. At Spokane House, Finlay spoke only French, and his sons knew about as much English as Douglas knew French. When he got ready for a trip into the Blue Mountains south of Walla Walla, Douglas explained the purpose of his trip to a trapper who translated the words into French for a Canadian interpreter who spoke to Douglas's Native American guide in his own language. After two hours of negotiation, involving considerable pipe smoking, a price was settled upon: food, shoes, a knife, a piece of cloth, and tobacco. Even so, the trapper sent along his twelve-year-old son who was able to talk with the guide but, Douglas suspected, never told either man exactly what the other said.

Winters were cold and dominated by rain and snow, and confinement dulled the senses. Douglas worked on his specimens, packaged his seeds, wrote his diary and allowed his body to slowly heal. In the spring of 1827, he decided to join a group of trappers traveling from Fort Vancouver to Hudson Bay. One can only imagine how thrilled the trappers were to have a botanist along who wanted to constantly stop and gather some weed or seed.

Travel up the Columbia was rapid, the party crossing the 49th parallel one month after they left Fort Vancouver. It took four months to traverse the Canadian wilderness, and much of that with Douglas on foot. Whenever he could, he walked along the river's edge and collected new plants. Occasionally he would shoot a small animal or bird to add to his growing natural history collection he was transporting in boats or on horseback. He gathered cones and seeds of the northern conifers whenever he could, but none of them was as spectacular as one he sought out in the fall of 1826.

For much of September Douglas was engaged in preparing his specimens for shipment to England and readying himself to go in search of the pine with the huge cone that he was told about in 1825. With a party of thirty, once again commanded by McLeod, Douglas left Fort Vancouver on the 20th and followed the Willamette River finding the low hills covered with the madrona named for Menzies. In early October, near the Umpqua River, he found chinquapin, *Castanopsis chrysophylla*, and California laurel, *Umbellularia californica*, along with at least two new species of birds. The fine salmon trout, already known from Lewis and Clark's collection, were eaten and enjoyed during the last week of October while accident-prone Douglas, once again lame and ill, recovered from his botanical efforts in a small village. The fish were augmented with laurel and hazel nuts, the latter the same species Marshall knew from Pennsylvania and named in 1785.

McLeod and his men pushed further to the south where they encountered

hostilities that resulted in the death of one trapper and the capture of the wife of one of the guides. He suggested to Douglas that he might wish to turn north. Douglas did so, parting with McLeod.

The 24th and 25th of October were days of traveling over broken ground and downed timber, exhausting both man and horse. The two nights of hail and thunder did little to allow time for rest. Even Douglas's small dog was foot-sore and tired. On the 26th, his guide and horse left in camp, Douglas climbed into the Umpqua River Mountains with his dog. Events of the day surrounding the discovery of sugar pine were briefly stated in his diary: "I put myself in possession of a great number of perfect cones, but circumstances obliged me to leave the ground hastily with only three—a party of eight Indians endeavoured to destroy me." In his field notes, he gave more details:

*A cone of sugar pine* (Pinus lamertaiana). *Douglas published only a few new species himself, most being named for him by other botanists. His short 1827 article on new conifers appeared in the* Transactions of the Linnean Society of London.

> The large trees are destitute of branches, generally for two-thirds the length of the tree; branches pendulous, and the cones hanging from their points like small sugar-loaves in a grocer's shop, it being only on the very largest trees that cones are seen, and the putting myself in possession of three cones (all I could) nearly brought my life to an end. Being unable to climb or hew down any, I took my gun and was busy clipping them from the branches with ball when eight Indians came at the report of my gun. They seemed to me anything but friendly. To save myself I could not do by flight, and without hesitation I went backwards six paces and cocked my gun. I was determined to fight for life. I stood eight or ten minutes looking at them and they at me without a word passing, till one at last made a sign for tobacco, which I said they should get on condition of going and fetching me some cones. They went, and as soon as out of sight I picked up my three cones and a few twigs, and made a quick retreat to my camp.

Today, Douglas's specimens, taken in haste from the mountains of southern Oregon and shipped to England, may still be examined at the Natural History Museum in London.

In Canada, Douglas traveled between Hudson's Bay Company posts: Jasper, Edmonton, Carlton, and Cumberland along the Saskatchewan River to Lake Winnipeg. By boat he traveled south to Fort Garry along the western shore and then to Norway on the eastern. The trip from Oxford down the Nelson River to York Factor on the shore of Hudson Bay was rapid in spite of his boat sinking in a rapid and having to spend time drying his collection. At sunrise on August 28, the party arrived at York Factor, safe. Douglas chides himself in his diary: "Why did you not bring *Gaultheria* alive—across the continent—2900 miles? It could be done."

Yes, he could have, but all of the other wonders he brought surely made up for this oversight.

Douglas arrived in London in October of 1827. He was ill for most of the crossing, having been caught on Hudson Bay for three days and two nights in an open boat. The aches and pains he suffered in the field, probably arthritis, returned in London with a vengeance; soon to be added were the uncertainties he felt about how his efforts would be received by members of the Royal Horticultural Society and his support within the Linnean and Royal societies. Feelings of inferiority plagued him almost from the moment he left the New World.

His English friends were pleased, and said as much. During the two years Douglas was in America, his shipments of plants arrived in London where, with the help of many, the seeds were planted and their products admired. As a result many new species were named for him, including several animals, among them the chickaree, the horned lizard, and the white-tailed deer. New American species introduced by him were soon appearing in botanical journals, their technical descriptions often augmented by colored illustrations. Douglas presented an account of his magnificent sugar pine in the *Transactions of the Linnean Society*, reading the paper in November of 1827. He named the new tree *Pinus lambertiana* in honor of Aylmer Lambert, patron to all of botany and an expert on conifers.

John Murray, the London publisher, asked Douglas to prepare his diary for publication with the blessings of the Horticultural Society. Previously, the Society had laid claims to all such writings, but in Douglas's case they felt it important to provide their collector with the honor and additional revenue. With the Society's secretary, Joseph Sabine, and its gardener and taxonomist, John Lindley, Douglas began to prepare the book. It was not to be. Douglas, already tired of London, yearned to leave. Sensing his frustration, the Society sent him back to Oregon. In October of 1829, he sailed for the Pacific Northwest and four more years of botanical adventures.

Left behind were hundreds of new species awaiting description. In time they would be accounted for. William Jackson Hooker described several in the first volume of his *Flora boreali-americana* published in 1829, and Lambert reported many of Douglas's new species of Pinus in 1832. The list reads like a who's who of western conifers for the name of David Douglas is tied to silver fir (*Abies amabilis*), grand fir (*Abies grandis*), white fir (*Abies lasiocarpa*), noble fir (*Abies procera*), Sitka spruce (*Picea sitchensis*), lodgepole pine (*Pinus contorta*), western white pine (*Pinus monticola*), ponderosa pine (*Pinus ponderosa*), and Douglas fir (*Pseudotsuga menziesii*). Still, the most magnificent is the pine that nearly cost him his life, the sugar pine, *Pinus lambertiana*.

*A cone of noble fir* (Abies procera).

M S del. J.N.Fitch lith.

Vincent Brooks,Day & Son Lt.<sup>d</sup> Imp.

# VII

# Monuments to a Distinguished Servant

*W*hat trees were to the estate grounds of the wealthy few, herbaceous plants were to the backyards of the common gardener. Even in the most unpretentious setting herbaceous plants expressed color and design; above all they gave pleasure to the curious. For a penny, one could enter the grounds of the Royal Botanic Gardens at Kew and walk among nature's products. Even small pots of flowers on a window shelf added brightness to otherwise drab scenes. The wildflowers of western Europe are numerous, but centuries of human occupation had lessened their numbers, and as always, what is common never seems to have the charm of the exotic.

With the ever-increasing role of annual border plants and low herbaceous perennials in formal garden design, the need for such plants for the wealthy became an important factor in the one-upmanship of European gardening. Of equal importance was their use in public gardens where, with careful selection, one could have flowers from early spring to late fall. Shrubs, selected for their flowers, shape, or the color of their foliage were increasingly wanted by gardeners. And, fortunately for the plant explorer, someone was always willing to make sure the curious and elegant plants from foreign shores were gathered at least for their garden.

David Douglas was not the only botanical collector in the American West of the 1820s. Aboard the *William and Ann* with Douglas in 1825 was Dr. John Scouler who was serving as ship's surgeon. Thanks to William Hooker, his former professor, and to John Richardson, who was then involved with the explorations of the Canadian Arctic, Scouler obtained an appointment with the Hudson's Bay Company.

Upon arriving on the Columbia River, the first plant the physician sought was sallal, the *Gaultheria shallon* of Pursh, recommended by

Menzies as a plant of potential value in the garden. The small plant, now commonly grown for its beautiful evergreen leaves, was found among the rocks of Baker's Bay at the mouth of the river. In the nearby forests, Scouler and Douglas found the rustyleaf mock azalea *Menziesia* that was soon to be a favored shrub prized for its leaves. On their first day of collecting in April of 1825 they found species of wake-robin and currants first gathered by Lewis and named by Pursh as well as numerous tiny mosses. In the following days around Fort Vancouver, Scouler found species of wild rose, blackberry, and several wild flowers. He even found *Linnaea borealis*, the circumboreal twinflower named for Linnaeus. All were to find their way into European gardens.

While Douglas remained at Fort Vancouver, Scouler returned to England by way of Vancouver Island. The island's meadows were a profusion of flowers and wherever the *William and Ann* dropped anchor, Scouler found bulbs and seeds to collect and live plants to carefully pot and bring on board.

Many of the plants he found had been gathered by Menzies, and in time would be found by Douglas. Still, when Hooker began to describe the new species from British North America, several proved to have been found first by Scouler, one of which, a delicate moss, he named Scouleria. Scouler's name was also associated with a catchfly (*Silene scouleri*), a St. Johnswort (*Hypericum scouleri*) and a mountain harebell (*Campanula scouleri*). All are occasionally found in the garden.

While Douglas explored the upper reaches of the Columbia River in 1826, two naturalists were sailing the Pacific Coast from Chile to Alaska as part of England's effort to discover the Northwest Passage. Since the days of Columbus, a northern route to the Pacific had been posited. John Cabot searched for it in 1497 for England's King Henry VII. Cartier, Drake, and Cook followed. Henry Hudson found the bay that bears his name in 1611, only to have further efforts curtailed when he was set adrift by a mutinous crew. William Baffin and then John Ross pushed further westward from the Atlantic. Overland routes were attempted. In 1770, fur trapper and explorer Samuel Hearne walked from Fort Churchill to the mouth of the Coppermine River, opening central Canada to the Hudson's Bay Company. Nearly two decades later, Alexander Mackenzie explored the country from the Great Slave Lake to the delta of the Mackenzie River, and in 1793, well before Lewis and Clark, he made the first trans-continental journey across North America. As both men found open water in the Arctic Ocean, it was reasoned that there might be open water between the two rivers.

From the Atlantic side in 1826, John Franklin and his men were exploring the region from the Coppermine River to the Mackenzie River delta. From the Pacific side, William Beechey was to sail to Kotzebue Sound and wait for Franklin at Chamisso Island. If Franklin did not appear in 1826, Beechey was to return in 1827.

With Beechey were naturalist George Tradescant Lay and ship's surgeon Alexander Collie. Their natural history studies were focused on the numerous islands in the Pacific with only limited effort devoted to continental North America. The *Blossom* arrived at Kotzebue Sound in late July and waited until mid October. Beechey sent a small party east along the coast to Point Barrow in August, with collections made whenever possible. With the threat of snow and ice, Beechey departed for warmer waters and arrived close to San Francisco in November.

Spain lost California along with the rest of Mexico in 1821. Mexico, the resulting new, far-flung nation was hard to maintain, the national treasury poor, and soldiers and administrators alike were discouraged with their isolated assignments on the northern frontier. For decades, the Spanish hold on upper California had been challenged. The mission system established from San José del Cabo in Baja California to San Francisco in Alta California was an attempt to establish a presence. While protective of their interests, the Spanish and even the Mexican governments were tolerant of foreign visitors to their Pacific ports as long as the objective was science, trade, or supplies.

Iris douglasiana.

While Russia had a firm hold on Alaska, England and Spain claimed much of the Pacific coast from there to Mexico. The presence of the Hudson's Bay Company on the Columbia River, and Spain's establishment at San Francisco Bay effectively defined the actual extent of their holdings. In the vacuum between Spain and England the Russians founded a settlement in California to supply their Alaskan outposts.

Steller's scientific finds off the coast of Alaska in 1741 revealed a diverse flora and fauna, and further explorations were undertaken. Under the direction of Czar Alexander the First, an expedition departed Copenhagen in September of 1803 on a five-year round-the-world voyage of discovery. With Captain Adam Johann von Krusenstern were Lieutenant Otto von Kotzebue and surgeon-naturalist Baron Georg Heinrich von Langsdorff. At Kamchatka, news that Napoleon had been declared emperor of France forced von Krusenstern and the bulk of the fleet to return to Russia. With Andrew Maschin in command of the brig *Maria*, von Langsdorff, along with former ambassador to Japan Nikolai Petrovich von Resanoff, sailed for Alaska in mid-June of 1805, visiting outposts of the Russian-American Company. In spite of Spanish promises to be cooperative, von Langsdorff was unable to do much in the way of collecting; his strong objection to the treatment of the enslaved Indian people probably did little to promote his cause.

At Sitka, the America vessel *Juno* lay at anchor under the command of "Northwest John" DeWolf. The New England captain sold his ship to the Russian-American Company in October. In February of 1806 von Langsdorff, as surgeon-naturalist of the ship went to Spanish California for stores. In March, on the very day Lewis and Clark started their eastward journey back to the United States, the *Juno* attempted to enter the Columbia River but failed. Landfalls were therefore few, and while von Langsdorff saw the great forests, he rarely was able to collect specimens.

At San Francisco, the Spanish welcomed the Russians although, with

Spain now at war with England, the *Juno* was first taken as an enemy ship. On March 29, the day after his arrival, von Langsdorff walked to the Mission where he was shown a small garden and encouraged to travel overland to the missions at San José and Santa Clara where, the mission fathers told him, wild flowers were in great abundance. Although he made a visit to San José, and the *Juno* remained in California until early May, von Langsdorff returned to Sitka without any plant collections. Nonetheless, he urged further scientific efforts in California, and von Resanoff urged a Russian presence north of San Francisco. To promote his political objective, van Resanoff promised to marry Concepción Maria Arguello, a daughter of the Commandant at San Francisco. Unfortunately, the ambassador died on his way to St. Petersburg in search of a formal appointment, and it was years before the young lady learned of his death. Although wooed by others, she died a single woman of eighty-seven having devoted her life to serving the poor.

With Russia's defeat of Napoleon in 1812 and his final loss at Waterloo in 1815, the Russian empire was ready to again conduct scientific explorations. In July, Otto von Kotzebue left Copenhagen aboard the *Rurick* bound for the Alaskan coast in search of the Northwest Passage. The ship's construction had been supervised by von Krusenstern at Åbo under the patronage of Count Romanzoff, Grand Chancellor of the Russian empire. Kamchatka was reached in mid-July of 1816, with the expedition continuing on to Kotzebue Sound and then to Unalaska.

In September, Kotzebue sailed for the warmth of California with naturalists Johann Friedrich Eschscholtz and Adelbert Chamisso, and artist Louis Choris. Eschscholtz and Chamisso collected seeds and a few plant specimens around San Francisco Bay during the month of October while the *Rurick* was being reoutfitted. In November, the crew sailed for Hawaii; there is no evidence that anyone visited the Russian outpost at Fort Ross (established in 1812) just to the north. The expedition visited several of the islands in the Polynesian group before once again heading northward in search of the Northwest Passage. When ill-health finally forced Kotzebue to abandon the effort in July of 1817, he returned to Hawaii, then crossed the Pacific to the Philippines and finally reached Copenhagen a year later.

The scientific results were impressive but delayed. In 1826, Eschscholtz published several of his new California species, three years after the manuscript was presented to the Imperial Academy of Sciences in St. Petersburg, and two years after Eschscholtz made his second trip to California. Earlier, in 1820, Chamisso described *Eschscholtzia californica*, the California poppy, and a new genus from Alaska that he named *Romanzoffia*.

On the second expedition with Kotzebue to California, Eschscholtz was much more successful with his botanical results. The Russian ship *Predpriatie* remained in California for nearly two months, departing San Francisco in late November. During this stay, the naturalist visited the missions at Santa Clara and San Rafael, venturing as far north as the Russian settlement at Bodega Bay and, by boat, a short distance up the

Sacramento River. He found several new species but their publication was so delayed that all were named by other naturalists.

From 1826 until 1829, the French ship *Heros* sailed the Pacific Coast in an effort to establish trading contacts. In 1827, the *Heros* visited most of the California ports from San Francisco to San Diego. The commander, August Bernard Duhaut-Cilly, was well received by the Mexican officials,

and his naturalist, Paolo Emilio Botta, an Italian by birth, was given complete freedom to collect. Botta was mainly interested in birds and reptiles, and while he gathered a few specimens named by Edouard Spach, the most notable being the California buckeye (*Aesculus californica*), his most interesting discovery was the roadrunner (*Geococcyx californianus*).

David Douglas left England aboard the *Eagle* in October of 1829, arriving seven months later at the mouth of the Columbia River. It was to be his last trip. From April of 1830 when he once again roamed the forests of "Northwest America" until he died in Hawaii in July of 1834, Douglas was a man devoted to the introduction of new species for the Horticultural Society of London.

In October, 1830, Douglas wrote Hooker that he spent much of July in the Blue Mountains of Oregon where he once again found his *Paeonia* and about a hundred other new species. In August, Douglas turned southward, ascending the Willamette River into the Cascade Mountains of central Oregon. On his return trip down the river in late September, he lost all of

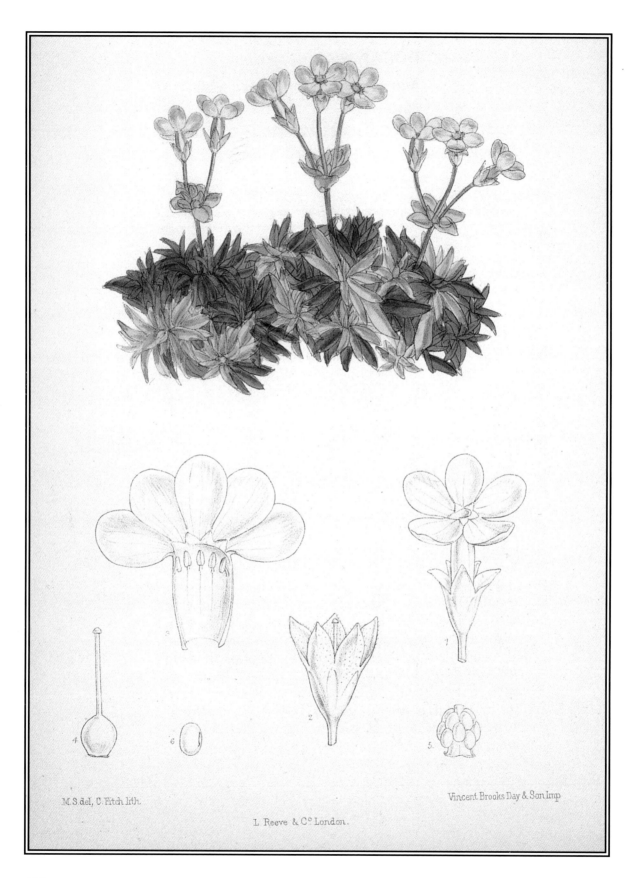

his zoological collections. In early October, when Douglas sent his letter to Hooker, he was unable to send the bulk of his dried plant specimens; instead he shipped three sea trunks filled with seeds. Nonetheless, he did send one bundle of six new species, including two new magnificent trees, the noble fir *Abies procera* and the grand fir *Abies grandis*.

While Douglas's letter and seeds made their way to London, he set out for California instead of Hawaii. He arrived at Monterey just before Christmas in 1830 with the idea of spending the winter months; in fact, he was unable to find a northward-bound ship until mid-August of 1832. Douglas might have been discouraged by his inability to return to the Pacific Northwest, but for botany and horticulture his long stay was a bonanza.

At Monterey Douglas lived with the English merchant William Edward Petty Hartnell, using this gentleman's linguistic skills and position to enable him to collect widely in the Mexican state. Upon his arrival, Douglas obtained permission to remain six months and later extended that to twelve.

*I*n a November, 1831, letter to Hooker, Douglas recounted that the first plant he collected upon his arrival in Monterey was *Ribes speciosum*, a plant found by Menzies and named by Pursh in 1813. At the same time, he found his first baby blue-eyes (*Nemophila menziesii*) that he told Hooker was certainly a "harbinger of Californian spring." The extent of the bounty coming that spring was soon evident. In April of 1831, Douglas journeyed overland to Santa Barbara, collecting in the mountains bordering the Pacific. In late June, shortly after his return to Monterey, Douglas set out for San Francisco, and spent July and much of August searching its rapidly browning hills, including Mt. Diablo, for plants. In all, Douglas sent to Hooker some 500 species that November, the vast majority new to science.

Among his finds were numerous herbaceous perennials of great interest to the gardener. He found several new species of mariposa lily (*Calochortus*), monkey-flower (*Mimulus*) and lupines (*Lupinus*). He found the bush poppy (*Dendromecon rigida*) and California fuchsia (*Zauschneria californica*), both soon to become part of the English garden flora. His search for great trees was rewarded by the discovery of the digger pine which Douglas asked be named *Pinus sabiniana* in honor of the secretary of the Royal Horticultural Society.

In Douglas's letter to Hooker he reported the arrival of Dr. Thomas Coulter, the Irish botanist who came to Mexico in 1825, and, while working at various mines, gathered thousands of specimens for Augustin and Alphonse de Candolle in Geneva. When Coulter arrived in late November, Douglas was delighted to have a kindred spirit. The two men fished and hunted together, and talked botany during the winter months of 1831-1832. Coulter walked to Santa Barbara in late March of 1832, following the Salinas River and visiting each of the missions. From there he continued southward, mainly along the coast, reaching the mission at Pala, near San Diego, at the end of April.

From here Coulter turned eastward, crossed the mountains, and

*(Left)John Lindley proposed the genus* Douglasia *in 1827 for a small, montane plant found on the talus slopes of the Cascade Range. Douglas made many efforts to reach the summit of Mt. Hood, and had he been successful, he would have found* Douglasia laevigata *, described in 1880 by Asa Gray.*
*(Above) The prickly phlox (*Leptodactylon californica*) was found by David Douglas on his overland trip between Monterey and San Luis Obispo. The plant was named by Hooker and Arnott in their report on the botany of the Beechey voyage.*

*Many of Douglas's plants gathered in California were named by others. The flat faced downingia,* Downingia pulchella, *was described by John Lindley in 1836.*

headed for the Ford of the Colorado River near modern-day Yuma, Arizona, which he reached on May 8th. He explored the rivervalley, sojourned to the mouth of the Gila River, and withstood temperatures that, according to his thermometer, reached 140°F. Throughout his trip, as well as during his return to Monterey, he collected plants.

In August of 1832, Douglas sailed on an American ship for Hawaii where he found the London-bound *Sarah and Elizabeth* willing to take on his two sea trunks filled with California plants. In this shipment, Douglas included many new species of mosses and sea algae, all bound for Hooker as these were of little interest to the Horticultural Society. There is no indication of what Douglas found that year, but he concluded in his letter to Hooker that in the nineteen months he was in California he probably found 500 new species. Today, most of Douglas's herbarium specimens bear a simple printed label: California, Douglas. 1833. The "1833" was the year the last of Douglas's California specimens arrived in England, and without any details about his travels in California in 1832, where he found them remains largely unknown.

Meanwhile, in California, Coulter continued to collect, but where he went, and even what he collected, is also unknown. He probably remained until late 1834 as in the following year he published an account of Upper California in the *Journal of the Royal Geological Society of London*. His large, personal plant collection of some 50,000 specimens representing more than 9000 species was, after some delay, finally deposited at Trinity College, Dublin, but Coulter's poor health prevented him from working on it. Adding to his depression was the loss of all his botanical manuscripts and his personal narrative, apparently stolen from the London to Dublin train.

Like Douglas, Coulter was interested in trees. In 1837, David Don, the librarian of the Linnean Society, described five new pines from California. One, the digger pine, he named *Pinus coulteri*.

David Douglas spent the last year of his life in the Pacific Northwest roaming the old-growth forests filled with the trees he named. His stay in Hawaii was a brief six days and his botanizing was limited by a "violent rheumatic fever" that kept him fretting near his bed. In late October, 1832, Douglas was once again at the mouth of the Columbia River, went up river to Fort Vancouver, and awaited spring. In March of 1833, Douglas made a rapid overland trip to Puget Sound, concentrating on the mosses and algae, obtaining some 200 hundred specimens of the former. In late March, back at the mouth of the Columbia, he headed northward by ship to northern New Caledonia as British Columbia was then called.

The collecting was rewarding, but on June 13, while riding in a small bark canoe on the cataracts of the Fraser River, Douglas lost every article he possessed except his astronomical journal, some rough notes, and his instruments. As he wrote Hooker from Hawaii in May of 1834: "My botanical notes are gone, and, what gives me most concern, my journal of occurrences also." He was 300 miles from any English outpost, without food, bedding, weapons, or collecting equipment. He emerged from the wild "greatly broken-down" and was soon "prostrate with fever" in the home of George Linton who, soon afterward, drowned with seven others in the same cataracts that nearly claimed Douglas.

By mid-July, Douglas was at Fort Walla Walla, once again searching the Blue Mountains for additional novelties. And again, Douglas failed to reach the summit of Mt. Hood. In October, Douglas left the Columbia River and made a slow trip by ship to California and on to Hawaii, keeping a new journal. The lateness of the season meant that he did "nothing in the way of Botany" while in San Francisco in November. He spent Christmas Day with the wife and sister of England's consul at Oahu, looking forward to a prolonged period of rest and collecting.

Douglas's efforts in Hawaii were richly rewarded. On Mauna Kea he found silver sword (*Argyroxiphium sandwicense*), and here and elsewhere an amazing array of ferns and flowering plants. As in the flora of western

North America, so the scientific epithet *douglasii* is frequently found in the flora of the Hawaiian Islands. He decided to concentrate on the islands' flora and use the excuse to recover his health. As he wrote to a friend about Mauna Loa: "One day there ... is worth one year of common existence." In his last letter to Hooker, written in May of 1834, Douglas indicated that he planned to remain on the islands until August or September and then return to England. He added a gentle prayer: "May God grant me a safe return to England."

It was not to be. In early July, Douglas left Oahu for Hawaii with the goal of climbing Mauna Kea. For some reason, he dismissed his guide and started across the mountain on the 12th. That day he fell into a bull pit and was killed by an entrapped bullock. When his body was found, his little dog was nearby still guarding his effects.

As with any mysterious death, theories abound. Douglas was last seen by an ex-convict, Edward Gurney, who became a suspect for the murder theorists. Douglas's eyesight was poor. He himself reported that he had lost all sight in his right eye, and the effects of snow blindness had affected the health of his left eye. Shortly before his death, Douglas wrote that the tropical sun caused him considerable pain, which was relieved only by "a slight discharge of blood from both eyes." Most forgot that Douglas was curious, and a bull in a pit, would certainly have attracted his attention. Accidents happen, and the history of Douglas in the field is filled with accidents.

The harvest brodiaea (Brodiaea coronaria) *(left) was named in 1808, but not in the garden until the 1830s. Douglas introduced into cultivation many species collected earlier by Archibald Menzies. The butterfly Mariposa lily* (Calochortus venustus), *(above) which is extremely variable in its coloration and markings, was introduced into cultivation by Douglas from California.*

The specimens Douglas found, and in many cases named, made their way to England. The Royal Horticultural Society distributed them to be formally published, and over the next decade Douglas's North American plants were described and illustrated. Most retained the names he suggested; many were named for Douglas as a tribute to and in recognition of his contributions to botanical explorations.

Douglas suffered a violent death, not an unheard of fate for botanical explorers. Yet, this is not Douglas's legacy. He discovered approximately one-third of the great western conifers and introduced into modern horticulture more than 200 species. His name was given to peaks, rivers, and even counties in Oregon and Washington.

In 1930, the Royal Horticultural Society erected a monument in Hawaii to honor "their distinguished servant" David Douglas. But cold, colorless stone can never replace the magnificent conifers and elegant shrubs and herbs he introduced into the horticultural world; those are Douglas's monuments, and no one can walk along the Pacific Coast of temperate North America without seeing and acknowledging their wondrous glory.

W. Fitch, del. et lith.

Vincent Brooks, Imp.

# VIII

# Western Gold, Botanical Style

*The Rocky Mountain columbine* (Aquilegia coerulea), *the state flower of Colorado, was found by Edwin James on Pike's Peak in July of 1820.*

The natural treasures gathered by Lewis and Clark and studied by Thomas Jefferson at Monticello in 1806—cutthroat trout, the prairie dog, the pronghorn antelope, and the grizzly bear—foretold the great natural wealth that awaited future explorers. Here, at least, was a tangible indication of scientific success.

In 1804, while Lewis and Clark worked their way around the Great Falls of the Missouri River, William Dunbar and George Hunter were organizing an expedition to ascend the Red River of the South. Delays meant that it was not until May of 1806 that it got underway, with Thomas Freeman in charge. Spain disputed the boundaries agreed upon by France and the United States and ultimately forced Freeman to return to Nachitoches. To the north, Zebulon M. Pike was readying his company to search for the head of the Arkansas River. The year before he had tried to find the headwaters of the Mississippi River, but the British prevented his success. Pike's 1806 expedition, while noted for the explorer's assault of a Rocky Mountain peak that would later bear his name, was, like that of Freeman's, curtailed by the Spanish.

The scientific results of these expeditions were disappointing. Freeman gathered a few natural objects, but Pike viewed the whole matter with contempt. In fact, it was Pike's labeling of the mid- and short-grass prairies west of the Mississippi River "The Great American Desert" that delayed westward migration for nearly thirty years. Jefferson firmly believed that it was imperative to explore and settle the new western lands, but the grim reports of the West convinced many that Jefferson's Louisiana Purchase was a folly.

Jefferson's fellow Virginian James Monroe, elected to the presidency in 1817, shared his dream of a settled West. The 1818 treaty with Great Britain, and another with Spain in 1819, settled the northern boundary of the

Louisiana Purchase and added Florida to an expanding United States. The latter also settled the southern and western boundary of the Louisiana Purchase, but to Jefferson, it was at a high cost. Spain was to retain all of Texas primarily because the question of slavery in the new southwestern territories proved impossible for the Americans to resolve politically. With the question of boundaries settled, it was again time for a president to call upon the Congress to fund new western explorations.

Major Stephen H. Long of the U. S. Army's Corps of Topographical Engineers had been on the frontier since 1817 selecting sites for military outposts. Their purpose was to protect America's interest in the fur trade and to control the Indian peoples. President Monroe, urged on by Jefferson and supported by Secretary of War John C. Calhoun, also envisioned a grand expedition to the Yellowstone—a vast, wondrous region first reported by the fur trapper John Colter in 1807 and known as "Colter's Hell." If a fort could be established along the Missouri River near the Mandan villages or at the mouth of the Yellowstone River, perhaps it would discourage the British from continuing their efforts to trap beaver along the whole of the upper Missouri.

In 1819, Colonel Henry Atkinson, with Long as his scientific aide, set off up the Missouri aboard steamboats. Along as botanist was William Baldwin. The trip was doomed from the beginning and Baldwin, already in poor health, died along with nearly a hundred others because of disease and deprivation. The political outcry was immediate and Congress refused to fund the rest of the expedition. Nonetheless, two minor efforts were approved, one to the upper Mississippi, the other to the Rocky Mountains.

*William Baldwin.*

Long assembled an excellent group of scientists. Thomas Say, destined to be a leading entomologist and ornithologist, was Long's zoologist. Replacing Baldwin was the twenty-three-year-old Dr. Edwin James, appointed to serve as botanist and geologist. Their assistant was Titian Ramsey Peale, the son of Charles Willson Peale, proprietor of Peale's Museum in Philadelphia.

The route across Pike's "Great American Desert" was direct. Up the Missouri River from St. Louis to Council Bluffs, and along the Platte River, following its southern branch to the base of the Rocky Mountains. For James, the "desert" was a land of bountiful flowers. In his diary he recorded species after species first found by Lewis and Clark and by Nuttall and Bradbury. Yet, he also recognized many to be new to science.

Once the expedition reached the Rocky Mountains, the flora changed, and James was impressed with the splendor of the towering mountains. In mid-July, he and two others climbed the tallest peak, taking two days to reach its summit. James collected all he and the others could carry. His comment at the time was direct: "Among the plants collected in this excursion, several appear to be undescribed." In honor of his feat, Long named the peak for James, replacing the name "Grand Peak" given to it by Pike. Neither would persist, and to the perpetual disgruntlement of naturalists, Pike's name is now associated with the highest peak in Colorado.

Long led his expedition south to the Royal Gorge of the Arkansas River and the southern boundary of the Louisiana Purchase. Yet, he continued, crossing Raton Mesa to the upper reaches of the Canadian River. They followed the river to Fort Smith, which they reached in late September. In spite of the lateness of the season and the rapid descent, James collected a good deal.

The botanical knowledge that James brought West with him was not accidental. Unlike the zoologist Say, who was self-taught, James, a graduate of Middlebury College, had been schooled by two of America's most respected naturalists, Amos Eaton and John Torrey.

*Stephen H. Long*

*T*he American Revolution dissolved more than just a governmental tie with Great Britain. The break in relations also forced the American scientific community to develop its own resources. The long-held dream of Barton to author a flora of North America was destined to fail, but his role as an educator was to succeed. His textbook, *Elements of botany*, first published in 1803, was used at the University of Pennsylvania and studied by the likes of William Baldwin, William Darlington and Eli Ives. In New York, David Hosack, who established the Elgin Botanic Garden as the first public garden in the United States, published his *Hortus elginensis* in 1806, and attracted a law student named Amos Eaton to his fold. Eaton's business dealings ultimately resulted in a four-year jail sentence, during which he taught botany to the son of the prison's fiscal agent, a young John Torrey.

The bond that formed between Eaton and Torrey was strong. In New York, Torrey studied medicine with Samuel Mitchell and botany with Hosack; graduated with his medical degree in 1818 at the age of twenty-one; and had a catalog of the plants about the city of New York ready to go to press.

When James returned from the Rocky Mountains, he began to work up his collection with the intention of describing the new species discovered by Baldwin and himself. Many were accounted for in Thomas Nuttall's new book *Genera of North American plants* published in 1818, and studied by James before his 1820 trip, it being an improvement over the floras published by Michaux and Pursh as well as Jacob Bigelow's 1814 *Florula bostoniensis* and even Eaton's 1817 *Manual of botany*. A few of the plants found along the Canadian River were in Stephen Elliott's new work, *A sketch of the botany of South Carolina and Georgia*, but most of those that were still new had been found the year before by Nuttall.

In 1819, Nuttall journeyed up the Arkansas River to Forth Smith, and from there, on foot and by skiff and flatboat, he explored several river drainages and nearby mountain ranges going as far south as the Red River. In 1821, Nuttall published an account of his trip, and in the *Journal of the Academy of Natural Sciences of Philadelphia*, he described several of the new species. A subsequent series of articles appeared in 1835 and 1836. Some of the new species were offered for sale at the Linnaean Botanic Garden in Flushing, Long Island, New York, operated by William Prince and his son.

With Torrey's assistance, James drafted descriptions of several of his new species; these appeared in his *Account of an expedition from Pittsburgh to the Rocky Mountains* published in 1823. Among them were the limber pine (*Pinus flexilis*) and the columbine destined to be the state flower of

Colorado, *Aquilegia coerulea*. Most of the five hundred-some species Baldwin and James gathered were studied by Torrey who, in a series of three papers published from 1824 until 1828, accounted for most of the new plants.

John Torrey was rapidly becoming America's foremost taxonomist. In 1824 he became professor of chemistry and mineralogy at West Point with the rank of Assistant Surgeon in the Army. In 1822, he published a catalog of the plants found by Professor David Bates Douglass of West Point who was a member of Governor Lewis Cass and Henry Rowe Schoolcraft's 1820 expedition to the headwaters of the Mississippi River. Torrey's North Carolina correspondent, Lewis David von Schweinitz, wrote a catalog of the plants Thomas Say found along the Red River of the North in 1823. Schweinitz and Torrey then wrote an account of the North American species of Carex in 1825. Previously, Schweinitz published papers on North American mosses and bryophytes, and in 1822, wrote the first major American work on fungi wherein he described some three hundred new species. His 1832 *Synopsis fungorum in America boreali* firmly established him as the "patron saint of North American mycology." Concurrently, Torrey was publishing *A flora of the northern and middle sections of the United States* followed by his *Compendium* treating all of the vascular plants north of the Potomac River.

*The Rocky Mountain raspberry (Rubus deliciosus) was found by James and named by Torrey in the* Annals of the Lyceum of Natural History of New York.

For Nuttall, who returned to America in 1815, collecting was his principal goal. With the desire to increase the number of American species in the horticultural trade, he visited the now elderly William Bartram for suggestions of where to visit in the South, and consulted with the nurseryman Bernard M'Mahon on what kinds of plants were popular. Nuttall was determined not to make his living setting type, but rather to sell plants and seeds. His first trip, in the fall of 1815, took him to the Potomac and Shenandoah rivers, and down the Blue Ridge. He sailed from Alexandria, Virginia, to Savannah, Georgia, where he visited William Baldwin who was destined to head west in 1819, despite his pulmonary weakness. Nuttall botanized along the Savannah River to Augusta and then worked his way through central South Carolina to Wilmington, North Carolina. In spite of his traversing ground already visited by the Bartrams, he found numerous new species that he named in 1818.

The following year Nuttall collected in western Pennsylvania and the Ohio Valley, meeting Dr. Charles Wilkins Short in Kentucky. Short, then practicing medicine in Lexington, would eventually become professor of materia medica and medical botany at the University of Transylvania and ultimately dean of the Louisville Medical Institute. A prolific collector, Short amassed an herbarium of approximately 15,000 specimens, many of which he sent to Nuttall and Torrey for identification and naming. Over the years he published a series of works on the flora of Kentucky. Later, in Charleston. Nuttall paid his respects to Stephen Elliott.

That fall, Nuttall made up a collection of ornamental plants, which he sold to various European gardeners as well as to M'Mahon and others in the United States. Proceeds did not cover all of his expenses, and in 1817 and 1818, Nuttall was once again confined to Philadelphia making a living setting type. One task was his own *Genera*. With Thomas Say, he helped establish a journal for the Academy of Natural Sciences, contributing articles as well as setting the type.

Preparing his *Genera* was frustrating. Authentic material for the American species named by Linnaeus, Michaux, Pursh, and others was in European herbaria and therefore unavailable for his study. A second problem was more local; it was Constantin Samuel Rafinesque-Schmaltz.

*B*orn in Constantinople of a French father and a Greek mother of German extraction, Rafinesque was a genius and a self-taught naturalist. His interests in the social, physical, and natural world were limitless, and over his lifetime he wrote nearly a thousand books, articles, and published letters. He came to the United States from Italy in 1802 and remained until 1804, returning in 1815 after a decade in Sicily. He amassed a huge herbarium, collecting widely in the United States. When Michaux's *Flora* was published in 1803, Rafinesque wrote a harsh review that Samuel Mitchell published in 1806 in the New York journal *Medical Repository*. Rafinesque bluntly stated, quite correctly, that Michaux had failed to account for many species and had misnamed many others. In 1815, Rafinesque published *Analyse de la nature* in which he classified all known living things in a natural system with many new family names. As he would bitterly and rightly complain, all of his fellow naturalists ignored this work, later proposing and receiving credit for names Rafinesque established in 1815.

Oenothera speciosa *was found by Nuttall in 1819 during his trip up the Arkansas River.*

In 1817, Rafinesque published *Florula ludoviciana*, the first effort devoted to the plants found in the Louisiana Territory. He would later maintain that he had considered accepting the position of naturalist on the Lewis and Clark expedition, but under what circumstances this "offer" was made is unknown. In each of his papers on botany, and particularly in his reviews of the floras and manuals published by Michaux, Pursh, Barton, Eaton, and others, Rafinesque proposed new names.

Rafinesque was a "splitter" in the sense that he tended to recognize more genera and species than were usually accepted by other naturalists. Torrey and Nuttall were appalled by the number of new names Rafinesque was reporting. In the end, Nuttall ignored most of what Rafinesque had to say, and set a pattern that would follow Rafinesque's botanical writings for more than a century.

Nuttall's book *Genera* was an innovation in the sense that, unlike the floras of Michaux and Pursh, his was in English, not Latin, and thus readily readable by most Americans. It was also concise and affordable. After his 1819 trip up the Arkansas River, and a series of lecture tours in 1820 and 1821, Nuttall became a professor of natural history at Harvard University in 1823. That fall, he and his students were in the field looking at birds, flowers, and minerals; when not in class, Nuttall was in Philadelphia talking botany with his friend Zaccheus Collins and ornithology with his comrade Thomas Say. Many of his sixty new genera were accepted by Augustin Pyramus de Candolle who was writing a new flora for the world entitled *Prodromus systema naturalis regni vegetabilis*. Illustrations of several species appeared in William Curtis's *Botanical Magazine*.

Life in Cambridge was dull. Nuttall made excursions to the White Mountains, corresponded with his friends, and wrote a textbook, *An introduction to systematic and physiological botany*. He was also engaged in writing the first volume of his *Manual of the ornithology of the United States and Canada*. Its success would make Nuttall as famous an ornithologist as he was a botanist. Still, it was not the same as collecting on the frontier.

*John Torrey*

At Harvard's commencement exercises of 1833, Henry Wadsworth Longfellow read a poem, but it is unlikely that Nuttall heard it. He was trying to finish the second volume of his *Ornithology* and wondering about his future. In 1830 Nuttall was forced to sell his herbarium to the Academy of Natural Sciences and his cabinet of minerals to the new University of Alabama. Fiscal conditions at Harvard were hardly sound, so that when Nathaniel Wyeth returned from Oregon with a small collection filled with new species, and a proposal that Nuttall go to Oregon with him in 1834, he seized the opportunity.

When Nuttall finished the second volume of *Ornithology* he turned his attention to Wyeth's plants, collected on his return trip from Fort Vancouver to St. Louis in 1833. After a brief visit with Torrey in New York, he went to Philadelphia to complete the task. He studied the first three parts of Hooker's *Flora boreali-americana* that contained many new species found by Douglas in the Oregon Country and Thomas Drummond to the north in Canada. On February 18, Nuttall's paper on Wyeth's plants was presented to the Academy by Charles Pickering, and in late March of 1834, it was printed in the *Journal*.

Nuttall would not see the published paper for two years because by then he was heading westward.

Traveling with Nuttall was fellow ornithologist John Kirk Townsend of Philadelphia. The two routinely collected together, Townsend concentrating on birds, Nuttall on plants. They reached St. Louis in late March of 1834, and after five days in the city they began a leisurely walking tour up the Missouri River collecting whatever caught their attention. At the end of April, with Wyeth and his company of seventy men and two hundred and fifty horses and mules, the two naturalists turned westward following the Kansas and then Big Blue rivers before cutting overland to the south bank of the Platte. On May 20, near the south fork of the Platte River, Townsend saw thousands of buffalo, and for three days traveled among the great animals. Tiny black gnats were in even greater numbers, their bites causing great pain, and leaving Wyeth's eyes swollen shut for two days.

Nuttall made every effort to stay ahead of the men and horses. Near

Chimney Rock in May, Townsend said Nuttall "was here in his glory." He also wrote:

> None but a naturalist can appreciate a naturalist's feelings—his delight amounting to ecstasy—when a specimen such as he has never before seen, meets his eye, and the sorrow and grief which he feels when he is compelled to tear himself from a spot abounding with all that he has anxiously and unremittingly sought for.

*Chimney Rock along the North Fork of the Platte River near Scotts Bluff, Nebraska, was a familiar landmark to many pioneers along the Oregon Trail.*

The region west of Fort Laramie was unlike anything Nuttall had seen during his previous trips to the Louisiana Territory. The high mountains surrounded him, and the short-grass prairie gave way to a plant community dominated by a sagebrush Nuttall would later name *Artemisia tridentata*, a species common to arid western North America. In early June the company left the Platte River and crossed over the Continental Divide to the Sweetwater River near Independence Rock upon which future pioneers would carve their names. When Nuttall and Townsend reached the "beautiful, clear, deep and rapid" Green River, each went in search of curiosities.

At the rendezvous on the Ham's Fork of the Green River, Wyeth discovered that William Sublette of the Rocky Mountain Fur Company refused to honor his contract to purchase $3000 worth of merchandise, but this did not prevent the usual amount of "swearing and screaming" and hard drinking common to all rendezvous. Townsend was appalled that a pint of hard liquor cost three dollars, to be paid for only in furs. Women were bought and sold, contests were held, and gambling was unchecked.

Townsend declined to participate, and instead went fishing, catching several new species, and Nuttall searched the barren, clay slopes for more new plants. When Wyeth and his party left for Oregon, about thirty Flatheads

*Artists frequently accompanied scientific expeditions into the West and illustrated plants and animals in their native surroundings. This drawing depicts the Great Salt Lake.*

and Nez Perces joined them, asking Wyeth to give them protection from the Blackfoot. In mid-July, on the banks of the Portneuf, Wyeth built an outpost he named Fort Hall. As this was going on, Nuttall and Townsend rested, put their collections in order, and added more new species. Three weeks later they were following the Snake River bound for Oregon.

The trip across the Snake River plains in the heat of August was trying for man and beast. The trail cooled only when the company moved up the Burnt River in eastern Oregon and into the large and beautiful prairie of the Grand Rounde surrounded by densely forested mountains. The Blue Mountains, which had so often beckoned David Douglas, were no less attractive to Nuttall and Townsend. This was explored country and the season was late, nearly September, and Wyeth was anxious to reach the Columbia. Still, outside Fort Walla Walla, he called a halt, and with Nuttall's razor, beards were removed, hair was cut, and clothes were changed.

Townsend and Nuttall, not entirely by choice, rode horseback down to The Dalles where they found boats to take them and their collections down to Fort Vancouver. The rain and wind were so violent on the Columbia River that the whole of Nuttall's plant collection was damaged by water. Once on shore, Nuttall stripped off all his clothes, built an enormous fire and proceeded to dry and arrange his plants, specimen by specimen, all the while "with great drops of perspiration" rolling off his brow. Already Nuttall had gathered more than a thousand specimens, most of which he felt represented new species.

When Nuttall and Townsend reached Fort Vancouver on September 16, they were met by the legendary Dr. John McLoughlin, the chief factor and long-time friend of Douglas. McLoughlin and Wyeth were in negotiations as to where the American would establish his operations, and the decision allowed Wyeth to build his outpost on the Williamette River. Nuttall and Townsend initially collected in the Williamette Valley, only to set off for Hawaii in early December of 1834 where they hoped, like Douglas before them, to spend the winter collecting in the comfort of a warm tropical sun.

The following year Nuttall and Townsend collected in the Pacific Northwest throughout the growing season. When the surgeon and sometime collector, Dr. Meredith Gairdner of the Hudson's Bay Company, went to Hawaii, Townsend assumed Gairdner's duties at the Fort Vancouver hospital until November of 1836. He then took passage on the *Columbia* bound for Hawaii and Chile. He returned to Philadelphia in mid-November of 1837.

*N*uttall spent the winter of 1835-1836 in Hawaii, but instead of returning to the *Columbia*, he took the brig *Pilgrim* to California. He probably visited San Francisco in late March before going on to Monterey. From there he went to Santa Barbara, San Pedro, and finally San Diego. Once at Monterey, he was able to collect freely, and discovered several species not yet found or described from Douglas's material. In Santa Barbara and San Diego, he gathered more than a hundred new species. At the latter port, Nuttall the naturalist became a minor character in a great American story.

When Nuttall sailed for Boston, he was aboard the *Alert* made famous in Richard Henry Dana's *Two Years Before the Mast*. In 1834, Dana had left Nuttall "quietly seated" in his chair at Harvard:

> ... the next I saw of him, [he] was strolling about San Diego beach, in a sailor's pea-jacket, with a wide straw hat, and barefooted, with his trousers rolled up to his knees, picking up stones and shells. ... The Pilgrim's crew christened Mr. N. "Old Curious," from his zeal for curiosities, and some of them said that he was crazy, and that his friends let him go about and amuse himself in this way.

Nuttall's western adventure was an enormous success scientifically, but it came at a price. To be away as long as he was he had to resign his position at Harvard so that when he reached Boston in late September of 1836, he had no future prospects. From 1836 until 1841, Nuttall worked at the Academy of Natural Sciences in Philadelphia, preparing publications on the plants, animals, and minerals he found in the West. It was a period of enormous productivity even if it was punctuated by periods of fiscal worry. The future of American botany was in the able hands of John Torrey, and Nuttall was all set to contribute his part to Torrey's newly proposed *Flora of North America*.

In September of 1830, Torrey received a letter from a young botanist then living in upper New York state who was studying at the Fairfield Medical School. He was clearly more interested in botany than medicine. The young man found Torrey's 1823-1824 *Flora* useful, and Torrey urged him to collect certain rare species in his area. Shortly after that, Torrey was studying a packet of plants sent by Asa Gray. The letters and parcels continued, and when the two finally met in 1832 Gray was teaching botany and mineralogy at the Bartlett School in Utica. In 1833 Torrey sailed for Europe where he spent five weeks in Glasgow, Scotland, talking over the future of North American botany with William Jackson Hooker, author of *Flora boreali-americana.*

That work was designed to cover the plants of British America, namely Canada and the Oregon Country. Hooker was completing the text of the first volume when Torrey suggested to him that upon his return to New York, Torrey commence a work on the plants for the whole of North America north of Mexico. Torrey used his trip to London and Paris to examine the collections made by Linnaeus, Clayton, Michaux, and Pursh as well as to examine material being sent by Douglas and Drummond. He also examined the western American plants gathered on the Beechey voyage, and with Robert Brown reviewed those from the arctic north of Canada and Alaska. Upon his return, he carried with him many duplicates of the more recently obtained American specimens.

To a great degree, Torrey's herbarium was rapidly becoming the major repository of American collections. Moses Ashley Curtis of North Carolina sent him boxes of plants as did others then collecting in the South. One plant sent to Torrey and Nuttall by Hardy Bryan Croom was a Florida gymnosperm named *Torreya* by George Walker-Arnott, Hooker's co-author of *The botany of the Beechey voyage.* In 1827 Torrey had left West Point to assume a position at the New York College of Physicians and Surgeons; in 1830 he began lecturing at Princeton. The professor of natural history at Princeton was Dr. Joseph Henry, destined to become the first Secretary of the Smithsonian Institution, and it was through him that Torrey tried to find a position for Gray. He failed, and Gray accepted the curator position at the Lyceum of Natural History in New York.

If Torrey could not have Gray as a fellow professor, at least he could be his professional colleague. Torrey's dream of a new North American flora had been encouraged by Hooker, but when he asked the out-of-work Nuttall to join him, Nuttall declined. Even when he asked Gray, the response was not immediate. Eventually, they came to an agreement and in 1835 they began to work on the text.

Gray's efforts were fragmented by his efforts to obtain a position at the University of Michigan, and when appointed, his duty of going to Europe to purchase books for the university library. By the time Gray sailed in November of 1838, he had completed about half the text to which Torrey added his portion to complete the first volume. Earlier, in July and October, the first half of the first volume of *A flora of North America* had been published. The remaining two parts of volume one were not published until June of 1840; the added time allowed Gray to correct the manuscript.

In 1837, Nuttall agreed to supply Torrey with descriptions of his new American species. Over the next fifteen months, Nuttall worked closely with Torrey and Gray, sending them descriptions and specimens of nearly 350 new plants. These were variously modified by Torrey and Gray, but the majority were adopted and published. The remainder of his Arkansas plants were described in a long article in the *Transactions of the American Philosophical Society* published in three parts during 1835 and 1836. The new western North American and Hawaiian species of the sunflower family (*Asteraceae*) were published in two 1841 *Transactions* papers.

Most of Torrey and Gray's *Flora* was written by Gray, Torrey acting more as an editor than an author. The arrangement worked well. When Gray returned from Europe in November of 1839, he discovered that serious financial difficulties in Michigan meant that he did not have immediate employment. Conditions did not improve so that when, in 1842, he was offered Nuttall's former position at Harvard University, he accepted. The text for most of the second volume of the *Flora* was complete, and the third and final part of the volume was printed in February of 1843.

*The vegetation on the deserts of the American Southwest and adjacent northern Mexico is dominated by members of the cactus family, and is the frequent subject of expediton artists.*

*R*umblings from Rafinesque continued to be heard. His 1825 work, *Neogenyton*, wherein he proposed sixty-six new genera of North America, was only marginally acceptable to his contemporaries. The 1828 *Medical flora* was widely used because its many colored plates were useful in the identification of medicinal plants. In 1836, Rafinesque began his *New flora and botany of North America* which was published in parts through 1838. In concert with that was his *Flora telluriana*. Both were filled with hundreds of new genera and thousands of new species. Many American trees and shrubs were reviewed in Rafinesque's 1838 *Alsographia americana* and his *Sylva telluriana*.

Torrey and Gray were appalled by Rafinesque's proliferation of scientific names and simply ignored most of what he published. Without specimens it was impossible to evaluate his work, and even his illustrated *Autikon botanikon* published in 1840, which was accompanied by specimens, proved unhelpful for they were unable to understand Rafinesque's species concept. Rafinesque left Kentucky for Philadelphia in 1825, but even Nuttall, who was in Philadelphia was unable to comprehend Rafinesque's many new genera and species. Few people in the East knew that Rafinesque had built a garden in Lexington containing some forty thousand plants and animal specimens, that he had been awarded a gold medal by the Geographical Society of Paris for his work on the similarities of the native peoples in Asia and America, or that he had distributed more than twenty-five thousand specimens of plants to mainly European herbaria.

While Rafinesque could be ignored, British botanical explorations along the Pacific Coast could not. The 1836-1842 round-the-world voyage captained by Edward Belcher brought two naturalists, the surgeon Richard Brinsley Hinds, and the gardener George Barclay to Northwest America in 1837. They collected from Nootka south to California where Hinds made a trip up the Sacramento River finding *Juglans hindsii*, a species of walnut now used as stock for budding English walnut. Their ship *The Sulphur* returned in 1839, reaching the mouth of the Columbia River at the end of July, and then sailed northward into Puget Sound. In September, the ship was in Bodega Bay near the Russian's Fort Ross, and then in San Francisco, Monterey, Santa Barbara, San Pedro, and San Diego. Hinds and Barclay collected when they could, but most of the curiosities along the immediate coast were

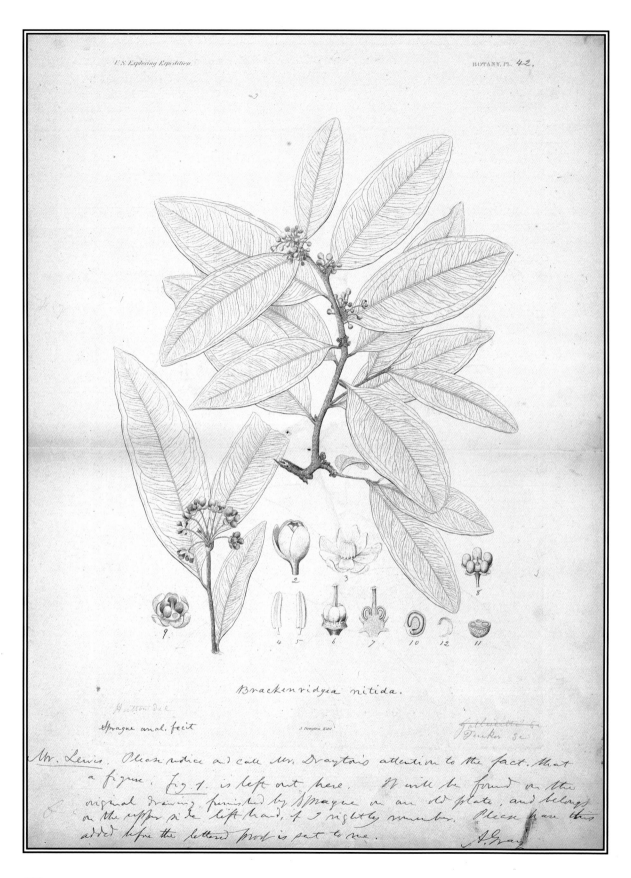

*Brackenridgea nitida.*

Hutton del.

Sprague anal. fecit

J. Drayton. 1841

Sartain Sc.
Jenkin Sc.

Mr. Lewis. Please notice and call Mr. Drayton's attention to the fact. that
a figure. Fig. 1. is left out here. It will be found on the
original drawing. furnished by Sprague on an old plate. and belongs
on the upper side left hand. if I rightly remember. Please have this
added before the lettered proof is sent to me. A. Gray

already well known. However, *The Sulphur* continued down the coast of Baja California, where the naturalists discovered many new species which George Bentham described from 1844 until 1846. Hooker also accounted for a few species in the second volume of his *Flora*.

Russian naturalists occasionally collected plants in California during the 1830s, with Admiral Ferdinand Petrovitch Wrangel sending seeds to St. Petersburg where they were grown, studied, and named by Friedrich Ernst von Fischer and Carl Anton von Meyer. The entomologist, Ilya Gavriloch Vosnesensky collected nearly 350 specimens in 1840 and 1841. Unfortunately, these were not studied until 1937, long after the novelties had been described by others. The Russian sale of Fort Ross to John Sutter in December of 1841 signified their last botanical effort in California. In Alaska, however, Russian naturalists collected plants and animals until the region was purchased by the United States in 1867.

For decades European nations had been sending large, scientific expeditions on extensive voyages around the world. In 1838, the United States launched its first such maritime expedition under the command of Captain Charles Wilkes. When Congress first authorized the expedition in May of 1836, several naturalists were sought. Thomas Say offered his services, and both Titian Peale and Asa Gray signed on. When the six vessels and its corps of scientists and artists finally departed two years later, the United States Exploring Expedition had lost Say and Gray, the latter's place taken by the "horticulturist" William Dunlop Brackenridge. The expedition, famed for its discovery that Antarctica was a distinct continent, did not reach the coast of western North America until April of 1841. Brackenridge initially botanized eastward to Coeur d'Alene in Idaho before turning south, traveling with Lieutenant George F. Emmons overland from the Columbia River to San Francisco. With the botanist on the two-month trip were Peale and the mineralogist James D. Dana.

Although Douglas and others botanized much of the area south of the Columbia, and Hinds made a brief but productive trip up the Sacramento River, the region in between was largely unknown. The season was late, but the collecting was good, and several new species were found.

When the Wilkes Expedition returned to the United States, laden with tens of thousands of specimens and artifacts from South America, the Pacific islands, and the Far East, there was no place to deposit them. There were volumes of data and thousands of illustrations, but there was no obvious place to publish. The botanical specimens (nearly ten thousand in all) went to Gray, and he described some non-American species in 1854. Seeds were distributed to various American gardens; unfortunately, few were able to handle the volume, and most of the species died. The failure to protect and preserve so many objects brought attention to the lack of a national museum. That was overcome when the Smithsonian Institution, founded by a bequest from the English scientist James Smithson, was established in 1846. Congress supported publication of some of the expedition's results, some not appearing until their scientific usefulness was considerably diminished. Torrey's comments on Brackenridge's American plants, for example, were not released until 1874.

*Charles Wilkes*

*Many new plants were found by the Wilkes expedition on the islands of the Pacific.* Geranium arboreum *(below), a large shrub, was discovered in the Hawaiian Islands. The botanical artist Isaac Sprague worked closely with the botanist Asa Gray on the illustrations for the Wilkes expedition reports, as may be seen by Gray's notes to the printer on a proof of Sprague's drawing of* Brackenridgea nitida *(left), a new genus named for the horticulturalist William Dunlop Brackenridge.*

Torrey did publish one new genus. In the new *Smithsonian Contributions to Knowledge* Torrey named *Darlingtonia californica*, the rare western pitcher plant found by Brackenridge on Mt. Shasta. A year later, in 1854, Gray proposed *Brackenridgea* for a Pacific island plant.

*Darlingtonia californica, the western pitcher plant.*

Botanical explorations in the 1840s were destined to be dominated by government-sponsored expeditions and an expansionary war. It was also a period dominated by the idea of a Manifest Destiny that the United States should be a nation stretching from sea to sea and from the Arctic Ocean to Panama. One champion was Senator Thomas Hart Benton of Missouri, and carrying his sword, was his son-in-law John Charles Frémont.

During his thirty-year tenure in the United States Senate from 1820 until 1851, Thomas Hart Benton was a vocal advocate of agrarian reform and westward expansion. He promoted free homesteads and land at reduced prices as an incentive to western settlement; he so vigorously supported a policy of hard currency that he was known as "Old Bullion" to his colleagues. His future son-in-law came to his attention when Frémont served with Joseph Nicholas Nicollet in 1838 and 1839 mapping the upper Mississippi River drainage and adjacent regions. The botanist for the expedition was the Saxon-born Karl Andreas Geyer who introduced Frémont to the art of making fine collections of plants. Geyer's collection was studied by Torrey who published his findings as an appendix to Nicollet's 1843 *Report*.

Frémont, the bastard son of an itinerate French language teacher and the young wife of an aged but wealthy Virginian, was destined to become one of America's most romantic heroes. In spite of the early death of his father and the stigma of his birth, young Frémont began work in a law office that allowed him to acquire enough of an education to enter the junior class at the College of Charleston in May of 1829 at age sixteen. His skill in mathematics brought him to the attention of Joel Robert Poinsett, the former minister of Mexico for whom Robert Graham of Edinburgh named the popular genus *Pointsettia* in 1836. Poinsett helped Frémont gain various positions in mathematics aboard naval ships and eventually, when Poinsett was Secretary of War, an appointment with the Corps of Topographical Engineers.

While working with Nicollet in Washington on the expedition's report, Frémont was in frequent contact with Senator Benton, and his second daughter, Jessie. At sixteen, Jessie was the delight of her father, and Frémont's attentions were not fully welcomed. Negotiations between Mrs. Poinsett and Mrs. Benton resulted in an agreement on a one-year postponement of an engagement. Neither of the young people could honor the postponement, and in mid-October of 1841, Charles and Jessie were secretly married.

Nicollet's health was failing, and when the senator finally learned of his daughter's marriage, he accepted the obvious and began to promote Frémont as Nicollet's successor. As a result, Frémont headed his first expedition in 1842, mapping the Oregon Trail from Council Bluffs to South Pass in Wyoming. In the Wind River Range he climbed the highest peak, which he named for himself. His guide was Kit Carson.

Botanically, Frémont was following a well-worn trail and only a few new plants were reported by Torrey in the expedition's 1843 report. The report itself, published by Congress, was carefully crafted and written with the help of Jessie. Unlike previous expedition reports, this one was filled with adventure, and to the reader it told of a new American hero.

Frémont's 1843-1844 expedition from the Missouri to the Columbia, then south into the Great Basin, across the Sierra Nevada in the dead of winter, and into the deserts of Nevada and Utah was to be one of the most important of all of the government's early expeditions. For Torrey and Gray it was also an exciting expedition though they could not find a botanist to send and Frémont took on the duties of naturalist. The account of Frémont's second expedition was published by the Congress in 1845; like the first, it was written with the help of Jessie Benton Frémont. For the reader, it was grand adventure.

The purpose of the second expedition was to continue the mapping of the Oregon Trail from South Pass to the Columbia. With Frémont were cartographer Charles Preuss, six of the men who went with him on the first trip, Louis Zindel, the Prussian artillerist, and as guides, Kit Carson and Thomas "Brokenhand" Fitzpatrick.

The start of the 1843 expedition was abrupt. In St. Louis, Frémont requested a small howitzer. As his expedition was supposedly a peaceful one, its presence was questioned. Learning that her husband would be summoned

*Poinsettia* (Poinsettia pulcherrima) *was named for Joel R. Poinsett, the first American minister to Mexico, where the plant is native.*

to Washington to explain, tradition has it that Jessie secretly sent Charles a note to depart immediately. Whatever the truth, Frémont left for Bent's Fort the evening of May 29 and the orders were never received.

After mapping the region along the eastern slope of the Rocky Mountains of Colorado, Frémont moved northward to the North Fork of the Platte, crossing the Continental Divide in mid-August. He followed the Oregon Trail to Soda Springs, then turned south to the Great Salt Lake where he remained until mid-September. While there, and using an "India rubber boat," he explored the islands, collecting a few plants and animals. The lateness of the season forced the expedition to make a rapid retreat to Fort Hall and across the Snake River Plains to Fort Boise, a Hudson's Bay Company outpost, and on to Fort Vancouver which they reached in early November. The expedition was fully engaged in mapping the whole of the area; Frémont himself was collecting plants while others concentrated on fossils, minerals, and zoological specimens.

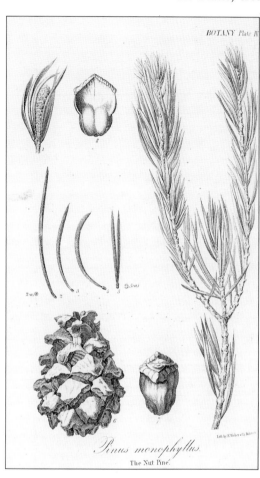

Many of the plants Frémont found had been collected previously by Nuttall when he followed the Oregon Trail in 1834. In 1843, Geyer, who had been with Frémont in 1841, also collected along the same route. After leaving Frémont, Geyer spent much of 1842 collecting plants in Illinois and Missouri for the St. Louis botanist George Engelmann. A physician by training, Engelmann arrived in St. Louis in 1833 where he had a successful practice. He was an early correspondent with Torrey and Gray, and with their encouragement, began describing new species and sending specimens to them. In 1843, Engelmann published a catalogue of Geyer's plants in the *American Journal of Science and Arts.*

Geyer's travels along the Oregon Trail were promoted by Hooker who was looking for more specimens from the interior of the Oregon Country. Geyer kept no diary, but his notes were published by Hooker in the *London Journal of Botany* in 1845 and 1846. The route taken across the "Missouri Territory" was up the Platte River to Fort Laramie, then over South Pass to the Sweetwater River. During this part of the trip, Geyer traveled with Sir William Drummond Stewart of Murthly Castle, Scotland. With Geyer were Stewart's own collectors, Alexander Gorden and Friedrich G. F. Lüders. Along as artist was Alfred Jacob Miller of Baltimore, another of the early painters of western American scenes. The plants and animals being sought were for the castle grounds, but in many respects, this was the first "pleasure party" to venture across the Missouri River. Stewart had made several westward trips with fur-trappers and traders since 1832, and the crimson-painted wagon canvas and tents, Persian carpets, and a horde of servants to make it all happen must have been quite a scene!

Upon leaving the Stewart party, Geyer joined a party of Jesuits going to

*The illustration of single-leaf pinyon* Pinus monophylla *(above)published in Frémont's* Report. *The Pacific dogwood* (Cornus nuttallii) *(right)was named for Thomas Nuttall by John J. Audubon in 1838.*

M. S. del J. N. Fitch lith.

Vincent Brooks Day & Son Ltd. imp

J. Reeve & Co. London.

their mission among the Flathead in western Montana. Here, in the fall of 1843, Geyer attempted to find passage down the Yellowstone River to the Missouri. John James Audubon, the famed zoologist, was then collecting birds and mammals along the Missouri River, going as far as the mouth of the Yellowstone. An occasional collector of plants who described *Cornus nuttallii*, the mountain dogwood on the Pacific Coast, he was traveling with the gifted scientific illustrator Isaac Sprague who illustrated many of Torrey and Gray's new species. Few new plants were found, but Audubon named the Missouri titlark for Sprague, reporting his artist to be an excellent shot.

*G*eyer turned westward from the Flathead mission in November of 1843, crossed the Bitterroot Mountains and passed the winter at the Chamokane Mission in present-day Washington. The following spring, after several short trips, Geyer reached the Lapwai Mission of the Reverend Henry Harmon Spalding and his wife on the Clearwater River in westernmost Idaho. The Spaldings, like the Reverends Elkanah Walker and Cushing Eells at Chamokane, were members of the American Board of Commissioners for Foreign Missions, a Boston-based group promoting Christian religion among Indian people. Geyer, who finally became such a pest that Mrs. Spalding insisted that he leave, instructed her in the art of making good botanical specimens. Over the next three years she gathered plants that her husband sent to Asa Gray, with the result that he received credit for her discoveries. The killing of Marcus Whitman, his wife, and eleven others at the Waiilatpu mission in November, 1847, by a band of Cayuse Indians caused all of the missions to close.

When Geyer sailed for England in November of 1844, he was laden with many new species of plants from the interior. The specimens found by Gordon were also soon before Hooker. Geyer collected so much material that Hooker was able to divide his plants into twenty different sets; these were offered for sale to other botanists. One of Gordon's plants was named *Atriplex gairdneri*, implying Meredith Gairdner found it. As for Geyer, his name is commonly encountered, having been given by Hooker and others to thirteen species, a fraction of the new plants he found.

Little is known of of G. F Lüders's collecting activities, but his fate and that of his collection was recorded by Frémont. In mid-November while Frémont making a portage around some rapids near The Dalles, Lüders arrived in a canoe. The two men spoke briefly before Lüders attempted to run the rapids. His canoe was swamped and all was lost—equipment, gear, and specimens—two years of work gone in an instant. In 1886, the historian Hubert Bancroft wrote of this incident:

> The toils and dangers of this class of men occupy but little space in history. ...It is a brave deed to dare the perils of the wilderness for those, in company of hundreds, but much nobler it is for the solitary student of science to risk life for the benefit of mankind.

Frémont assembled his expedition at The Dalles and plotted a course homeward. They would proceed south searching for the Buenaventura, a great river that early Spanish maps prominently displayed, running from the wastes of the Great Basin to the Pacific. By following that river into California, they could easily pass through the Sierra Nevada. From there, they would follow the Old Spanish Trail into Utah, over the Rocky Mountains, and back to St. Louis.

The bleakness of the cold desert in December burdened the men

*Frémont and his men near Carson Pass in the Sierra Nevada during the winter of 1844.*

and animals. By the end of January, Frémont was convinced that the Buenaventura was mythical, and he decided to cross the Sierra Nevada. On the 24th, a man presented him with a small bag of seeds belonging to a local species of pine. Frémont dutifully collected specimens of the single-leaf pinyon that he and Torrey named *Pinus monophylla*.

The expedition entered the Sweetwater Mountains where, on January 29, 1844, the twelve-pound howitzer was cached by Preuss near the base of a steep hill just north of Cottonwood Meadow along Cottonwood Creek. Finding what is now a branch of the Walker River, they continued northward until they came to the Carson River; this they followed upstream and westward. The snow was deep, the food low. In early February, while climbing the steep slopes of the Sierra Nevada, a mule fell to its death carrying to the bottom of an inaccessible canyon nearly all of the scientific collections made since Fort Hall. Upon reaching the summit food was so scarce that the camp's dog, Klamath, became dinner. The desolation of rock, snow, and even higher peaks was obvious as the company looked out on the great Central Valley and Carson recognized the distant Coast Range; it was little consolation. On the 14th, Frémont and Preuss climbed a high peak and looked upon a beautiful lake entirely surrounded by mountains; it was to become known as Lake Tahoe, taken from the Piute word "Tah-ve" for snow. For days the men labored to get themselves, animals, and supplies to Carson Pass, and the task was not completed until the 20th.

March in the Central Valley brought a gold profusion of pleasant blossoms, the California poppy named for Eschscholtz. Little did Frémont realize, as he rode along the American River, that there was yet another kind of golden profusion awaiting discovery. Sutter's Fort was a needed respite; the host was generous, the food plentiful, and soon the company was ready to continue its way home. The trip down the Central Valley in late March was rapid and rewarding. Flowers were everywhere. In mid-April they crossed the Tehachapi Mountains and entered the Mojave Desert where Frémont encountered several new plants. Everywhere he turned, he found something new to collect.

The route along the Old Spanish Trail was not entirely unknown botanically. In the fall of 1841, William Gambel, a Philadelphia friend of Nuttall's, followed the route from Santa Fe to Los Angeles with the Workman-Rowland Party. He collected several new species of plants and animals, and his name is today associated with Gambel's oak (*Quercus gambelii*) and the Gambel or desert quail (*Lophortyx gambelii*). Gambel's plants, however, would not be named by Nuttall until 1848, so that all Frémont saw was still new to science.

The route eastward, across Nevada and Utah into the Rocky Mountains and out onto the plains of Kansas, was a hurried one with little time to collect. Then, on the night of July 13, 1844, the Kansas River suddenly flooded camp, "the baggage was instantly covered, and all our perishable collections almost entirely ruined, and the hard labor of many months destroyed in a moment."

In the days and weeks following Frémont's return to Washington he was engaged in organizing his notes, distributing specimens—plants to Torrey, fossils and animals to James Hall, the New York State paleontologist—and urging Preuss to complete the maps. Frémont took a particular interest in the plants he collected and requested that he be allowed to describe the new species with Torrey. Frémont's name would be attached to many other species over time. Gray described the new ones belonging to the sunflower family, five of which represented new genera; one he named *Nicolletia* for the late Joseph Nicollet.

*The fame of frontier scout "Kit" Carson grew considerably due to the many dime novels in which he was the hero. In real life, Carson was a knowledgeable guide, Indian agent, and an officer in the Civil War.*

With Jessie's help, Frémont's *Report* was submitted to Congress and published in March, 1845. It attracted considerable attention, especially among those interested in settling in the West and following the route outlined by Frémont to Oregon. His descriptions readily dissolved the myth of "The Great American Desert." The dense conifer forests, rich valley bottoms, clear and clean water he depicted revealed a West far different from the impression left by Pike. In the future, families would travel west with Frémont's *Report* in hand.

The strain in the relationships between the United States and Mexico continued after the deaths of William Travis, James Bowie and Congressman Davy Crockett, along with nearly two hundred others, at the Alamo in 1836. In 1845 Benton, always a keen observer of events along the western border, realized that the strain was nearing a breaking point, and war was likely. Who better to be in California, should war begin, than Frémont.

*T*he events leading to the Mexican War of 1846 were founded in the cultural differences between the two nations, the almost religious belief that American-style democracy should be imposed on all other nations in the New World, the question of slavery, and the failure of Mexico to pay its foreign debts. The fact that the nation's "Manifest Destiny" could be furthered by the capture of Texas and California is a point that cannot, and should not be ignored. The American-dominated population of Texas, even after the Alamo, continued to call for independence, while in California, impatience with Mexican rule became evident among the ever-increasing number of Americans.

Frémont's official orders for his third expedition were to establish the point, on the Arkansas and Red rivers, where the 100th meridian formed the western border of the United States. He later received permission to detach a group, which was headed by Lieutenant James W. Abert, to explore south into New Mexico. It now appears that he also received oral instructions to proceed westward to California so "as to ascertain the lines of communication through the mountains to the ocean..." notes Frémont in his autobiography.

Frémont reached Bent's Fort in August of 1845, ordering Abert south into New Mexico over Raton Pass and then eastward across the panhandle of Texas and Oklahoma to the Canadian and Arkansas rivers. Abert dutifully collected plants, but little of significance was found. Frémont, with Carson, Fitzpatrick, and later Joseph R. Walker as guides, ascended the Arkansas River, crossed the Rocky Mountains to the Great Salt Lake, and crossed the Great Basin to the base of the Sierra Nevada. Shortly after entering Nevada, Frémont divided his party, sending Walker with the topographer and artist Edward M. Kern, under the command of Theodore Talbot, southwest across the desert following the Walker River, past Walker Lake and over Walker Pass (all names suffgested by Talbot and formalized by Frémont) into what is now Kern County, California. A smaller party of fifteen men remained with Frémont; they went due west over the Sierra Nevada in late November.

Frémont's actions in California were both confrontational and prudent. In early March of 1846, he and his men were ordered to leave California; his response was to build a fort in the Gabilan Mountains near Monterey only to withdraw on the pretext of exploring a route from California to Oregon.

The likelihood of war was also bringing others westward. By the end of June, 1846, one month after war was declared on Mexico, Colonel Stephen W. Kearney was ready to leave Fort Leavenworth with his "Army of the West," bound for Santa Fé. He was in command of some 2700 men, nearly all of whom were mounted. In July, the five-hundred-strong "Mormon Battalion" volunteered and was added, lagging behind the main force. The small Mexican villages in New Mexico were captured without hostilities, the Mexican commander of the region having been encouraged to leave by an American trader and friend of Senator Benton. Leaving a portion of his army to administer New Mexico, and sending a second into Chihuahua, Kearney set off to capture California. With him was a company of topographical engineers under the command of Lieutenant William H. Emory.

Botanists were seemingly everywhere. Engelmann's friend and medical partner in St. Louis, Dr. Frederick Adolphus Wislizenus, was botanizing in

*The snake lily* (Dichelostemma volubilis) *was first found by Karl Theodor Hartweg who collected in California after Douglas from 1846 until 1848. The stems twine through shrubs.*

Mexico when he was taken prisoner by Colonel Alexander William Doniphan. Wislizenus collected on the Santa Fe Trail, and along the Rio Grande south to El Paso, but his most worthy plants were found when he was under house arrest around Cosihuiriachi in Chihuahua. The results were summarized by Engelmann in the botanical appendix of Wislizenus's *Memoir of a tour to northern Mexico* published in 1848. Also in northern Mexico at the time was Josiah Gregg, author of *Commerce of the prairies* (1844). He and the army physicians often collected on the battlefields, perhaps an effort to take their minds off the carnage. Engelmann in Wislizenus's *Memoir*, and later Torrey and Gray, accounted for most of the new species found by Gregg.

*Fannel bush* (Fremontodendrom californica) *was named by Torrey in* Smithsonian Contribution to Knowledge. *Fremont found the plant near the source of the Sacramento River in the northern Sierra Nevada in April of 1846.*

Around Santa Fé, Augustus Fendler was botanizing. After living in the United States and Texas for several years, Fendler was encouraged to collect plants by Ernst Meyer, a professor of botany at the University of Königsberg. Encouraged even more by Engelmann, Fendler arrived in Santa Fé two months after Kearney claimed the area for the United States. That fall and winter, Fendler collected widely in northern New Mexico, getting into the higher and more isolated mountain ranges. Among his new plants was the subalpine fir, *Abies concolor*. In 1849, Gray wrote his "Plantae fendlerianae novi-mexicanae" published in the *Memoirs of the American Academy of Arts and Sciences*, where he proposed the new genus *Fendleria* in honor of Fendler.

The route Emory took to California was across the Sonoran Desert, a vast area unexplored botanically. A keen observer and a talented officer, he was well suited to collect what he could, when he could as Kearney moved his Army to California. The season was unfortunately late, but what there was often proved to be novel. Many of the large, desert shrubs had been found by Frémont and were already known to Emory. The numerous cacti attracted his attention, and the giant saguaro was an obvious one to collect. When Torrey later examined Emory's collection, he found several species he knew would soon be described by Dublin's William Henry Harvey in Dublin and Gray using Coulter material found in 1832. Harvey, interested in algae, was in the United States in 1849 and 1850, working on a series of publications for the Smithsonian Institution on the marine algae gathered on the Wilkes Expedition. One of their new genera was the desert sunflower *Baileya*; this was proposed in Emory's 1848 *Notes of a military reconnaissance*. In this work, Engelmann presented an extensive review of the cacti, many of which were illustrated.

In June of 1846, war came to California when, with Frémont's help, the Americans began the Bear Flag Revolt against the local Mexican government. While in Oregon in April, Frémont received instructions from President Polk, the nature of which are unknown. They were delivered by the President's special agent, Archibald H. Gillespie, who rode north from San Francisco to find the explorer. In addition to conveying orders which he had memorized, he also carried letters from

Benton. Whatever the combination of information might have been, the response was swift.

After the Americans seized arms and ammunition in Sonoma, along with several prisoners, they met on July 4. Accepting Frémont's advice, they declared their independence and formed the Bear Flag Republic. With a force of 150, Frémont set out to conquer the rest of Alta California, unaware that the United States had formally declared war against Mexico in May. At Monterey, he joined forces with naval Commodore Robert F. Stockton. The retreating Mexican force was cut off in Los Angeles, and forced to retire into Old Mexico. By early December, however, the Mexicans had regrouped, and when Kearney and his "Army of the West" reached San Pasqual near San Diego, they attacked. Over the next month there were a number of running battles. Finally, along the Los Angeles River in early January, 1847, Kearney finally defeated the small Mexican force.

Frémont and Stockton had already established a civilian government, and Stockton of the navy had appointed Frémont military governor. Kearney objected, Frémont supported Stockton, and General Kearney immediately placed Captain Frémont under arrest. Kearney's defeat at San Pasqual, with the loss of eighteen killed and thirteen wounded (among them Kearney), was in stark contrast to Stockton and Frémont's success with minimal losses. At the end of May, Frémont left California under house arrest. The court martial began in November, and at its conclusion, John Charles Frémont was found guilty of disobedience and mutiny and dismissed from the army. Within days, President Polk accepted the findings of the court but suspended all punishment and restored Frémont's sword. Nonetheless, the captain resigned, his role as an explorer, naturalist, and soldier seemingly ended.

Little did Frémont realize that in a few months gold would be found in the mill race of a sawmill being built on the South Fork of the American River for John Sutter, nor could he guess the importance that his surveyed routes to the Pacific would play in the gold rush of 1849. The future would find Torrey describing several of Frémont's newly found plants. Frémont was to become the first Republican presidential candidate in 1856, a failed general in the Civil War, a territorial governor, and a man dying in near poverty.

And little did Torrey and Gray appreciate that the United States was now a nation stretching from the Atlantic to the Pacific, and that there were still many more new species to be discovered. Their long-delayed *Flora of North America* was always on their mind. Only a few more discoveries and they could return to writing text; only a few more expeditions and most of the novelties would be found. It was not to be. Gold would tie the nation together east-west, and war would tear it apart north-south.

*John Charles Frémont*

W.Fitch, del et lith.

Vincent Brooks Day & Son, Imp.

# IX
# Naturalists on a Disappearing Frontier

GOLD! The word does have an electric quality. The find by James Marshall and his workmen was soon known on the streets of San Francisco and within weeks digs were being worked all along the American River. Word of the discovery was reported by President Polk in his message to Congress in early December, 1848, and by mid-January, 1849, ships bound for California were filled with eager miners; sailors often deserted their ships when San Francisco was reached. Many of the less fortunate went overland, following Frémont's route over the Oregon Trail to the Mother Lode. Others took the more southern route surveyed by Emory, departing from Fort Smith in Arkansas.

The hazards of the trail were numerous under normal circumstances; for the inexperienced they were often fatal, and when cholera became a member of the party, death became the norm. Fresh graves dotted the trails, the carcasses of dead horses, mules, and oxen were simply allowed to rot. In 1850, more than fifty thousand men, women, and children followed the Oregon Trail, settled scores of rapidly developing mining towns. In that year, California became the nation's thirty-first and most isolated state.

Among the many were a few naturalists. William Gambel returned West, bound for the gold fields in 1849, only to be caught in the snow of the Sierra Nevada; he died in December of typhoid fever. John Woodhouse Audubon, son of the famed ornithologist, arrived from Texas in late 1849. With him was Dr. John Trask, one of the co-founders of the California Academy of Sciences, who later distinguished himself as a geologist, paleontologist, and botanist. Another to arrive that year was Dr. Jacob Stillman who sent a small collection to Torrey. Among the '49ers was the English botanist, William Lobb, an employee of the nursery firm owned by James Veitch of Exeter; it would be Lobb who would find the largest botanical nugget in the gold fields of California.

In August of 1833, Joseph Walker, who would later returned to California with Frémont, had encountered "some trees of the red-wood species, incredibly large—some of which would measure from sixteen to eighteen fathom round the trunk" on the lower slopes of the Sierra Nevada. If he mentioned his find to Frémont, it was not acted upon. In the spring of 1852, a hunter named Dowd found the tree in Calaveras County, and furnished Dr. Albert Kellogg of San Francisco with sterile specimens. The one Kellogg sent to Torrey was lost in the mail; a second reached Gray, but the specimen was so incomplete, he could not provide it with a name. Kellogg also showed a specimen to Lobb.

Realizing the significance of what he saw, Lobb headed for the Calaveras grove of big trees in 1853. He gathered seeds, herbarium specimens, and seedlings. While there Lobb saw one fallen tree to be nearly three hundred feet long with a diameter of more than twenty-nine feet. Back in San Francisco, he immediately departed for England, secretly carrying his discovery. These he gave to London's John Lindley who, in the Christmas day issue of the *Gardener's chronicle* proposed *Wellingtonia gigantea* for the "greatest of the modern heroes," the Duke of Wellington who died in 1852.

For Kellogg, who had hoped to name the massive tree for George Washington, a fact known to Lobb, this was an abridgement of all professional courtesy. Gray wrote Hooker lamenting Lobb's actions, calling into question the generic distinctiveness of the big tree when compared with the coastal redwood. Meanwhile, huge specimens of the tree were soon on public display, and trees were cut down merely to show that a naked trunk could be used for a dance platform.

The nomenclatural history of the two giant California trees, the coastal redwood and the big tree, would occupy the attention of botanists for another century. The coastal redwood was first collected by Archibald Menzies in the 1790s, but not named until 1828 when the English gentleman, Aylmer Lambert, proposed *Taxodium sempervirens* in the mistaken belief that it was closely related to the bald cypress of the Atlantic coast. In 1847, the Austrian phylogenist Stephan Endlicher proposed *Sequoia* for the redwood. The year after Lindley named the big tree for Wellington, the Belgian botanist Joseph Descaisne at the Musée Nationale d'Histoire Naturelle in Paris reduced *Wellingtonia* to synonymy and proposed *Sequoia gigantea*. This name was used by Americans (Europeans, and especially the British, continued to recognize *Wellingtonia*) until 1939 when the American, John Buchholz of the University of Illinois, demonstrated the distinctiveness of the big tree and proposed *Sequoiadendron giganteum*. Another genus had been named for Wellington before Lindley used it for the California tree, and thus his *Wellingtonia* was an improper name. By 1939, *Washingtonia* was the name of the desert palm native to California and Baja California so that Kellogg's name was not available. Today, the two trees are each accorded their own generic name given by a European to honor the Cherokee leader, Sequoyah, who saw neither tree.

*The rare California ladyslipper* (Cypripedium californicum) *was found by Albert Kellogg on Red Mountain in Mendocino County and named by Asa Gray in 1867. The big tree* (Sequoiadendron giganteum) *(right).*

After Frémont returned in disgrace from California, Torrey and Gray were occupied with his specimens. With the settlement of the Mexican war, a boundary survey became necessary and naturalists were needed. To this end, John Bigelow, Charles C. Parry, George Thurber and Charles Wright were appointed.

In 1848, Torrey received a letter from Parry, a former student of his at Columbia who sent him a small collection and asked if he knew of another position. Parry's tour with the Northwest Geological Survey, headed by the geologist David Dale Owen, was coming to an end, and he found botany much more interesting than medicine. Torrey responded by having him appointed to the Mexican Boundary Survey headed by William Emory.

6650

*The lemon lily* (Lilium parryi).

Parry's fellow botanist, Charles Wright, found his position thanks to Gray. Wright, a graduate of Yale, came to Texas in 1837 where he taught school, made surveys, and collected plants, sending his efforts to Gray. During the winter of 1848-1849, Wright was working for Gray in Cambridge, and the invitation to return to Texas and collect for Emory was readily accepted. In 1849, Wright traveled across Texas from San Antonio to El Paso. In 1851 and 1852, he gathered plants along the Mexican border from Texas to Arizona largely independent of Parry who was working the boundary in Arizona and California.

The botanical results were significant. Torrey wrote "Botany of the Boundary" for Emory, with Engelmann contributing the cacti. Parry introduced their contributions when the Report was finally published in 1858. Several of Torrey's sixty-one illustrations were done by Isaac Sprague, but Engelmann's seventy-five figures of cacti were drawn by Paulus Roetter and printed from steel engravings made in Paris. Among the new plants was the Mexican genus *Emorya*. In California, Parry found the rare *Pinus torreyana*.

Gray described many of Wright's new species in "Plantae wrightianae," with the assistance of Torrey and Engelmann. It was published in two parts (1852, 1853). As the final part was being published, Gray wrote Hooker that he "never had a collection so rich in entirely new things." Isaac Sprague illustrated several of the seven new genera and more than eighty species. Also included in the work were several of the new plants found by Gregg and Fendler. In 1854, Gray published several of Thurber's new genera and species in "Plantae novae thurberianae" in a volume of the

*Memoirs of the American Academy of Arts and Sciences.* While some of the novelties were found in California and Arizona, most came from Sonora, Mexico.

The year 1849 also found Howard Stansbury of the Corps of Topographical Engineers exploring the Great Salt Lake. Most of his travel was along the Oregon Trail, now crowded with gold seekers and a few Mormon families bound for Utah. Torrey summarized Stansbury's botanical efforts in an appendix to his *Exploration and survey of the valley of the Great Salt Lake* published by the Senate in 1851; it was illustrated by nine fine plates, but the name of the German artist is unknown. The lizard, *Uta stansburyi*, which is near the base of the food chain in the cold desert of the Great Basin, was named for the explorer who also collected specimens of the Mormon cricket.

To the south, Captain Randolph Marcy and Lieutenant James H. Simpson of the Fifth Infantry escorted a wagon train of prospective miners following the route generally traversed by Emory from Fort Smith to California. With Simpson acting as naturalist, several curious plants were found, including *Echinocactus simpsonii*, an elegant cactus named by Engelmann. Also on the trip were Edward and Richard Kern whose lithographs illustrate Simpson's 1850 *Report* showing the ancient ruins at Canyon de Chelly and Chaco Canyon.

Simpson argued that the route from Fort Smith to Albuquerque, and from there to Zuñi, was ideal for a transcontinental railroad. In 1851, Colonel John Abert, head of the Corps of Topographical Engineers, sent Captain Lorenzo Sitgreaves into the field with orders to explore the route from Zuñi across northern Arizona to the Colorado River. The surgeon-naturalist was Dr. Samuel Woodhouse who, because of various medical difficulties, spent more of his time tending the wounded than collecting novelties. Fortunately for natural history, a rattlesnake bite on his hand rendered him useless as a surgeon and allowed him to collect several specimens of birds and plants. Sitgreaves collected many plants as the expedition followed the Colorado River from the Mojave villages to Fort Yuma.

Communication with California was a national imperative, and from 1850 until 1862 the question of how that was to be achieved was argued in Congress and the nation. Even the questions of states' rights, slavery, and the dissolution of the United States occupied less of the nation's attention than where the most practical route for a railroad lay to California.

The initial proposals for a transcontinental railroad were formulated in 1845. With the acquisition of the Oregon Country in 1846 and the Mexican Accession in 1848, along with the final annexation of Texas, the land, at least, was available. The discovery of gold made a solution to the problem an immediate necessity. The congressional sessions from 1851 until 1853 were dominated by the subject. The political solution? A study.

In March, 1853, Congress called upon the Secretary of War "to ascertain the most practicable and economical route for a railroad from the Mississippi River to the Pacific Ocean." Secretary Jefferson Davis, later to

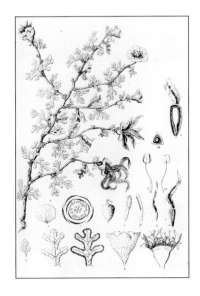

*The illustrations of tesota or Arizona ironwood (Olneya tesota), (below) and Stansbury's cliffrose (Cowania stansburiana), (above) demonstrate the maturation of botanical artistry in the United States where technical illustrations showing the fine detail of the flowers and fruits became standard for scientific reports after 1850.*

M.S.del. J.N.Fitch lith.

Vincent Brooks Day & Son Imp

L.Reeve & Co. London.

become Confederate President, effectively isolated Abert and his Corps by appointing Emory head of an independent Bureau of Explorations and Surveys to conduct the railroad surveys. To satisfy the sectional interests in Congress, four expeditions were organized.

The northern one was to explore a route between the 47th and 49th parallels, or from the Great Lakes to Washington state. It was headed by Isaac Stevens. Zoologist James Graham Cooper was appointed naturalist, and served as surgeon and meteorologist. His botanical efforts were minimal and their significance limited by the many discoveries made by the host of early naturalists who had explored the Pacific Northwest.

A central route, along the 38th parallel, was promoted by Benton who filibustered to have Frémont appointed its leader. Davis refused and Captain John Gunnison, who had served with Stansbury, was given command. It also appears that Davis wanted Benton's favored route shown to be impractical. With Gunnison was the German naturalist Frederick Cruezefeldt who had been along a portion of the route when Frémont went on an arduous midwinter expedition in 1848-1849 over part of the proposed route in the Rocky Mountains. Cruezefeldt managed to collect only 124 specimens before he, Gunnison, Richard Kern, and five others were killed by Utah Indians in October, 1853, near Sevier Lake. Assuming command was Lieutenant Edward Beckwith, who, the following year, surveyed the route from Salt Lake to the Sierra Nevada. His collector was James A. Snyder. The botanical efforts were modest, with Torrey and Gray naming a number of new species in 1857, including *Viola beckwithii* and *Gilia gunnisonii* to honor the two military officers.

Along the 35th parallel, one of the two more southerly routes, Lieutenant Amiel Weeks Whipple followed the route surveyed by Sitgreaves. Whipple had served on the Mexican Boundary Commission, and his trip from San Antonio to California during 1853 and 1854 included several scientists. Serving as botanist was John Bigelow who had collected on the Mexican border from 1850 until 1852. Bigelow was an excellent collector, but the lateness of the season in 1853 meant his contribution of novelties was limited. That changed when the party reached California. Also with Whipple was the artist and topographer Heinrich Balduin Möllhausen whose later novels on the American West would popularize many western myths for European readers. Torrey described the new plants in the second volume of the railroad reports, proposing *Whipplea* for a new genus of California plants related to Torrey's *Carpenteria* described in one of Frémont's reports; *Jamesia,* which Torrey and Gray named; and *Engelmann* and *Gray's Fendlera.*

Davis did not intend to send a survey along the 32nd parallel. As a Southerner, he was adamant that this was the only possible route, and there was no need, therefore, to bother with sending a survey to ascertain the obvious. Congressional pressure eventually forced him to dispatch Lieutenant John G. Parke and Captain John Pope, each in charge of a separate expedition, across different portions of the route from New Orleans to San Diego. To assure a snow-free route, an area south of the Gila River was obtained from Mexico in 1853, the route championed by

*Asa Gray*

*Frémont found the beautiful shrub (left) while crossing the Tehachapi Range in April of 1844. Torrey named the tree anemone (*Carpentaria californica*) to honor a Louisiana professor William Carpenter.*

James Gadsden, the minister to Mexico who negotiated the purchase. Interestingly, Torrey's report on the botany of the Parke expedition, with its eight plates, was available as a pre-print in 1856, more than a year before the entire work was published. Torrey and Gray collaborated to write a report on the plants gathered by Pope.

*The firecracker flower (Dichelostemme ida-maria) was found by a stage driver in the Trinity Mountains of California and named for his young daughter.*

O ther expeditions were dispatched to complete portions of the route to California. Lieutenant Robert S. Williamson explored the southern passes in the state discovering, as is the case today, that for the route between Yuma and San Diego to be completed, it would have to enter Mexico. He also surveyed routes across the San Gorgonio Pass into Los Angeles, and the Tehachapi and Walker passes into the southern San Joaquin Valley. With Lieutenant Henry L. Abbott, Williamson surveyed two possible routes leading into the Pacific Northwest.

The physician-naturalist assigned to Williamson's expedition was the 1846 University of Maryland graduate Adolphus Lewis Heermann. An excellent collector, he provided the Smithsonian Institution with 1200 bird specimens gathered from 1849 until 1852. It was Heermann who coined the word "oology" to denote the study of birds' eggs. His 1853 plants were described by Elias Durand, a French botanist working as a pharmacist and botanist out of his drugstore in Philadelphia, and Eugene Hilgard, then a chemist at the Smithsonian Institution who later gained fame as a soil scientist. Their report was published in 1854. Several of the new species came from the desert region of southern California.

Durand's work had in western botany continued with articles on a collection made by Henry Patten at Nevada City, California, and Utah plants sent to him by Jane Carrington whom Durand identified only as a "Mormon lady." With her specimens, and those found by Frémont, Stansbury, and Beckwith, Durand prepared a flora of the plants in northern Utah in 1859. Durand also obtained the herbarium of Rafinesque who had died in abject poverty in 1840. Unfortunately, Durand discarded most of the specimens so that today modern systematists have little direct knowledge of the plants Rafinesque described as new species. Consequently, the many scientific observations of Constantin Rafinesque continue to be ignored.

With Williamson and Abbott was John Strong Newberry, ultimately a colleague of Torrey's at Columbia when, in 1866, Newberry accepted the professorship in geology and paleontology. On Mount Lassen, Newberry found the elegant *Penstemon newberryi* named by Gray in the sixth volume of the railroad reports published in 1858. Also found was *Hemitomes*, a new genus of small, fleshy saprophytic flowering herbs that lack chlorophyll.

The obvious scientific success of the many volumes of the railroad reports did not resolve the political question of the most practicable route for a transcontinental railroad. But neither were they the only source of botanical novelties coming to the attention of Torrey and Gray. Local collectors in the South and West continually brought new species to their attention, and American collectors, instead of sending their specimens to London or Paris for identification, were sending them to New York or Cambridge. The new Smithsonian Institution also began to attract botanists and collections. Set aside but not out of mind was Torrey and Gray's *A flora of North America*. The persistent arrival of new plants continued to prevent Gray from taking up his pen to prepare the text for a third volume; he was particularly aware that by now the first two volumes were badly outdated, and their revision was imperative.

The failure of Congress to resolve the railroad question meant that

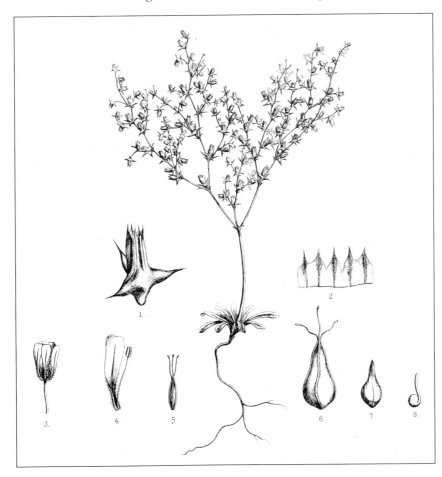

*The small annual herb* Centrostegia thurberi *was found by Dr. George Thurber during the Mexican Boundary Survey. The name of the new genus was proposed by Asa Gray and published for him by George Bentham in Alphonse de Candolle's* Prodromus *in 1856. This kind of cooperation was typical among botanists in the early and mid nineteenth century.*

future government-sponsored surveys of the Corps of Topographical Engineers would concentrate on wagon routes. The need to move the mail and freight remained a national priority as the 1850s came to a close, and funding for explorers and naturalists was forthcoming. Surveys were made of the Colorado River by Lieutenant Joseph Christmas Ives in 1857, and in 1859, Captain John M. Macomb tackled the San Juan River from its headwaters in the Rocky Mountains to its mouth at the Colorado River. The naturalist on both expeditions was Newberry. Ives was the first to follow the Colorado River into the Grand Canyon, and many botanical novelties were discovered. More important were Newberry's geological observations. The wagon road survey across the Great Basin by Captain James Simpson in 1858 demonstrated the practicality of this route even in the winter season. With Simpson was the geologist Henry Engelmann who completed the geological survey from the Great Plains to the Rocky

Mountains. The younger brother of George Engelmann, Henry gathered plants, a few mentioned in Simpson's 1859 report.

In April of 1860, the pony express began along Simpson's proposed route; in October of 1861, telegraph wires were connected in Salt Lake City effectively ending one of the more romanticized episodes in western American history. Overland mail also followed this central route, taking eighteen days to move from St. Joseph, Missouri, to San Francisco when the weather was reasonable and the roads neither muddy nor snow-packed. The great Concord coaches, pulled by four or six well-matched horses, readily moved passengers in the 1860s. More stagecoaches were robbed and drivers shot in the movies of the next century than during the whole of the era in the West. And more mail was carried by the pony express across the motion picture screen than the small group of men and fast Indian ponies ever moved.

*Charles Darwin*

*Our Lord's candle is the common name given to* **Yucca whipplei,** *a plant of the chaparral in California, named by Torrey for Amiel W. Whipple who explored the 35th parallel for the railroad surveys.*

The debate in Congress over western railroads was overshadowed masked by the ugly debate over the future of the nation. The election of Abraham Lincoln provided the excuse for South Carolina to secede from the Union, and within weeks, other states joined its lead. When war began in April of 1861, explorers became commanders and naturalists became physicians. Finally, without a southern lobby, a railroad was built from Omaha to Sacramento, and the decade-long debate came to an end.

The task of mapping and surveying the American West was largely over. The contributions of the naturalists and geologists were suddenly taking on a new importance with the publication, in 1859, of Charles Darwin's *Origin of Species*. The relationship of extant plants and animals with extinct forms seen in the fossil record was given meaning when placed in the proper geological sequence. Gray, an avid proponent of Darwin's thesis in America, demolished the creationist views held by his Cambridge colleague Louis Agassiz following his study of Japanese plants collected by Commodore Matthew Perry in 1853. In 1859, Gray showed an unequivocal floristic relationship between the plants of Japan and southeastern North America that could be explained only by geological and evolutionary processes.

The importance of geology had not escaped the attention of those planning the railroad surveys. In addition to reporting on rock formations, the likelihood of valuable minerals, and the general nature of soils, geologists also provided useful information for those interested in rich farm soil and productive grazing lands. Farmers and ranchers followed the soldiers who built forts and provided a degree of protection; with the discovery of gold came businessmen interested in providing services. That those services were often in the form of saloons and houses of ill-repute is a given; mercantile stores, churches, and reasonable forms of government, which also arrived on the frontier, are sometimes overlooked.

In California, where geology was fundamental to the economy, a geological survey of the state had its origin in the mind of Josiah Dwight Whitney in 1848. In 1853, John Trask was asked to submit a geological

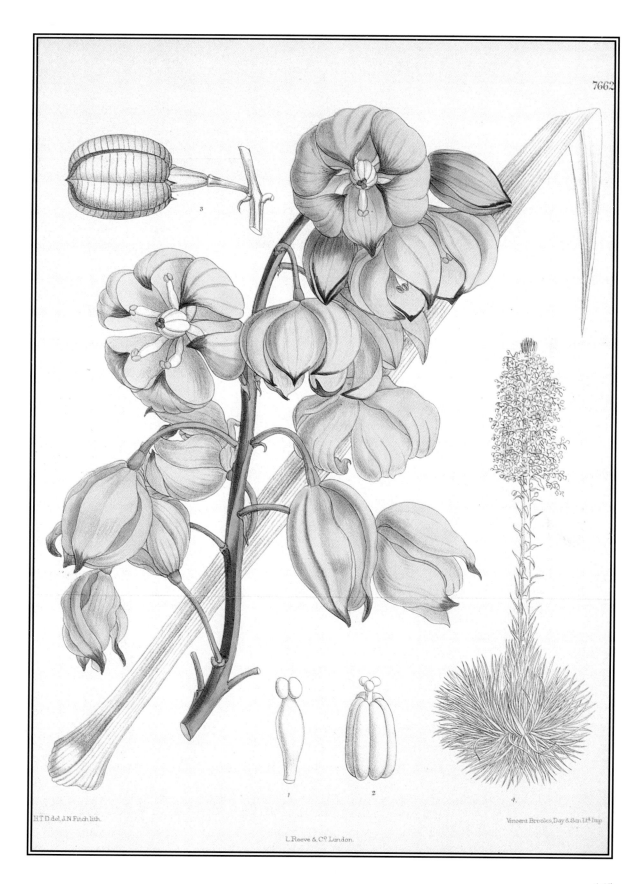

H.T.D.del, J.N.Fitch lith.

Vincent Brooks,Day & Son Ltḍ Imp

L.Reeve & Cᵒ London.

report to the state senate. His brief work, published in 1856, dealt with the Sierra Nevada, although he actually never visited the region. The geologists with the railroad surveys added much that was previously unknown, but still their observations were fragmentary. In 1859, Whitney called upon Agassiz and Dana, among others, to support legislation to form a geological survey then under consideration by the California legislature; in April, 1860, it was approved.

The Geological Survey of the State of California set out not only to describe and map the state's geological features, it was also to report on its botanical and zoological resources. Hired as botanist was William Henry Brewer.

Brewer, Yale educated, first tried to go West as botanist for the Gunnison expedition. His arrival, with Whitney, in California in November of 1860 set the stage for a series of intense botanical surveys. His efforts were rewarded with the discovery of many new species. A beautiful weeping spruce from the high mountains of northwestern California and adjacent Oregon was named *Picea breweriana*. Along the crest of the Sierra Nevada one can find many grasses, sedges, and wildflowers named for Brewer. A few were named for Whitney, although his name is best remembered for the Sierra Nevada peak that is the highest point in the contiguous United States.

*(Above) The San Gabriel firecracker* (Penstemon labrosus)*. (Above right) Surveyors in the field during the Whipple expedition in the 1850s. Western scenes (below right) were featured on many maps and itineraries as travel across the American continent became more common in the 1860s.*

*O*f considerable importance to the botanical success of the California Survey was the California Academy of Sciences. The Academy was established in 1853 and had seven founding members. Although its first president, Dr. Andrew Randall, was shot by a gambler in 1856, the organization rapidly grew. One of the founding members was Dr. Albert Kellogg who came to California in 1849. He botanized extensively in Alaska during the summer of 1867, and made frequent trips through California, even visiting several of the coastal islands. He made numerous illustrations of the plants he found, and published his observations in the Academy's *Proceedings*. His frequent field companion was William G. W. Harford whose interests were primarily in conchology.

Most naturalists who came to California sought out Kellogg. In 1852, John Jeffrey collected seeds and plants for a group of English supporters who established the Oregon Committee and funded his Oregon Expedition. Jeffrey collected mainly in northern California and in adjacent Oregon, but few of his efforts reached England. In early 1854 he set out for Yuma but disappeared, leaving no trace or tale of his fate. While on Mt. Shasta, he collected the large pine that now bears his name, *Pinus jeffreyi*. The French naturalist Ezechiel Jules Rémy arrived in San Francisco in 1855, traveling to Salt Lake City before returning via the Old Spanish Trail. A few of his novelties were described by Gray years later. The following year, Thomas Bridges, who had been collecting in South America and introduced the magnificent waterlily *Victoria amazonica*, arrived in California. He found the bright, red-flowered *Penstemon bridgesii* of the Sierra Nevada, but the bulbs of the spectacular *Lilium washingtonianum* named by Kellogg for George Washington failed to reach

England when the steamer *Central America* was lost at sea. Bridges made several trips into the interior of California over the years, occasionally visiting with William Lobb, who returned to the state in 1854 and was living in San Francisco. Lobb found and sent to Hooker seeds of *Torreya californica*, a species Torrey named from a specimen sent to him by a "Mr. Sheldon" who is otherwise unknown. Hooker, unaware of the name Torrey had assigned,

called the plant *Torreya myristica*, fixing the common name California nutmeg to this rare conifer.

Brewer's efforts in California were limited to four years. In 1864 he was replaced as State Botanist by Henry Nicholson Bolander. He collected throughout much of California as had Brewer before him. Bolander made an early botanical trip to Yosemite Valley, finding several new species and one new genus, which Gray named *Bolandra* in 1868. He was interested in mosses, and collected thousands of the tiny plants for study. His small *Catalogue of the plants growing in the vicinity of San Francisco* published in 1870 was one of his last botanical contributions; in 1871 he became State Superintendent of Schools and served in that capacity until 1875.

*W*hen Clarence King, one of Whitney's assistants, looked eastward from the crest of the Sierra Nevada in 1866, he saw the need for a survey across the Great Basin following the 40th parallel. The construction of a railroad across the nation had started, with thousands of men, at that very moment, laboring to lay track on the western slope of the Sierra Nevada. A detailed geological survey along the proposed route from the eastern base of the Sierra Nevada to the Rocky Mountains in Wyoming was reasonable, and in early 1867, King was in the field. How he obtained a military appointment and the necessary funding is still unknown.

As botanist King appointed William W. Bailey, the twenty-six-year-old son of the West Point scientist Jacob W. Bailey, and as zoologist he appointed an even younger Robert Ridgway, then just seventeen. When illness forced Bailey to return East after nine months in the field, the task of plant collecting fell to one of King's more able camp workers, the dishwasher and mule packer Sereno Watson.

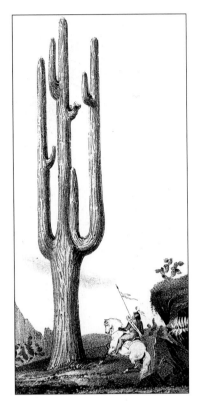 

Watson arrived barefoot in King's camp in 1867 and worked with Bailey. The following year, Watson collected in many of the mountain ranges of northern Nevada. In the spring of 1869, Watson and Ridgeway collected around Great Salt Lake, revisiting the islands where Frémont had botanized twenty-five years earlier. By August, Watson was in the Wasatch and on the northern slope of the Uinta mountains, finding many new kinds of plants. In September, he headed eastward from Green River, Wyoming, traveling on a train that since May had carried passengers and freight across the continent.

When Watson arrived in Cambridge with his plants, Gray found a shy man of unmistakable energy with a talent for things botanical. A graduate of Yale who had studied medicine in 1846, Watson had practiced in Quincy, Illinois, for two years. When he gave

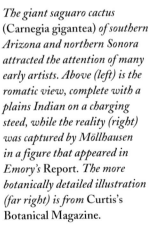

*The giant saguaro cactus (Carnegia gigantea) of southern Arizona and northern Sonora attracted the attention of many early artists. Above (left) is the romatic view, complete with a plains Indian on a charging steed, while the reality (right) was captured by Möllhausen in a figure that appeared in Emory's* Report. *The more botanically detailed illustration (far right) is from* Curtis's Botanical Magazine.

that up, he turned to teaching school, traveling from state to state almost at whim. His arrival in California had little purpose beyond curiosity, and his joining the King party was nothing more than another of his many jobs. For part of the summer when he was in the Utah mountains, Daniel Cady Eaton, grandson of Amos Eaton, was a fellow collector. It was Eaton, a recent graduate from Yale (1857) and a student at Harvard, who encouraged Watson to take his collections to Gray.

Sereno Watson was precisely the kind of person Asa Gray had been hoping to find. With Gray's help, Watson began to work up the specimens gathered by himself, Bailey, and Eaton. Watson's report of some five hundred pages on the botany of the King expedition appeared in the fifth volume of King's *Report of the geological exploration of the fortieth parallel* published by the federal government in 1871. The number of new species he described was truly staggering. Gray, Eaton, and other specialists who studied particular genera found many novelties they named for Watson.

At the same time, Watson took over from Gray many of the routine duties of running the large herbarium at Harvard University. He was also assigned the responsibility of dealing with the seemingly endless flow of

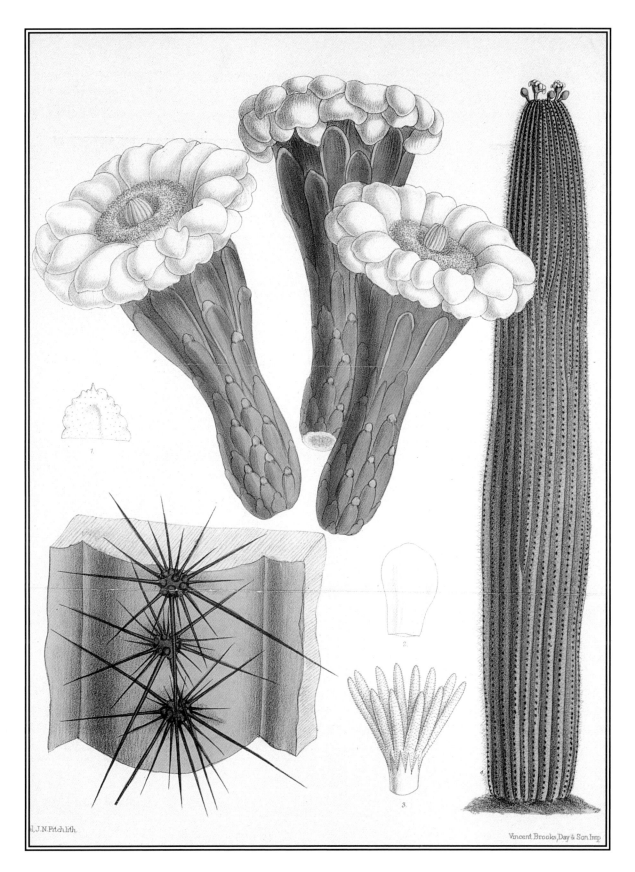

Vincent.Brooks,Day & Son.Imp

new plants coming in from the American West, and its associated correspondence. Watson embraced the task with enthusiasm, allowing Gray to consider retirement with the expressed purpose of returning to his *Flora of North America*. Events would make it impossible.

Just before Gray retired in 1873, John Torrey died in New York. The *Flora of North America* would never be finished. In his final years, Torrey was studying the wild buckwheats, a complex group of plants that included the genus *Eriogonum*, one of the largest genera of plants in North America. It had been a favorite of Torrey's since James brought him specimens from the Rocky Mountains in the 1820s, and he shared his observations with England's George Bentham who summarized the group in 1856 for de Candolle's *Prodromus*. With the discovery of numerous additional species during the many western surveys, Torrey turned again to the buckwheats with Gray's help. In 1870, Gray wrote a text and published a paper on the buckwheats granting Torrey senior authorship. It was a fitting tribute.

A detailed flora of North America was no long feasible, and Gray began a synoptical treatment. He finally had the time to devote to the project, and in addition to Sereno Watson, he had the help of a new generation of taxonomists: John Merle Coulter, William Farlow, George Goodale, and

Charles Sprague Sargent. Even so, collections continued to pour into Cambridge with novelties the expected rule rather than the exception.

In the West, the role of the army as an outlet for scientific exploration and discovery was coming to an end. Civilian agencies were being formed, and smaller, more scientific expeditions akin to that organized by King were taking to the field. Like King's, the expeditions organized by John Wesley Powell and Ferdinand Vandiveer Hayden had a predominantly geological focus. The army, not to be forced from the field, responded with its geographical surveys west of the 100th meridian.

Lieutenant George Montague Wheeler's charge was to topographically survey the region south of the Central Pacific Railroad from the deserts and mountains of southern California across Nevada and northern Arizona to the Great Plains of Colorado and New Mexico. The 1871 season was the most productive for Wheeler and his men. Assisting him were Grove Karl Gilbert, destined to be one of America's finest geologists, and Joseph T. Rothrock, botanist. The results of Wheeler's efforts over the decade from 1869 until 1879 are still impressive: the survey of nearly 150 mountain ranges, the profiling of more than 200 passes, the determination of the elevation of some 400 peaks, and the collections of more than 61,000 specimens. The results were published in some forty volumes, with the majority of those relating to biology concentrating on zoological disciplines. The sixth volume contained Rothrock's botanical report, but few new species were reported because most of the novelties had been described previously by Gray and Watson.

The surveys of Powell were largely supported by private monies with help from the Smithsonian Institution, while those of Hayden were sponsored by the Department of the Interior, an agency of the federal government established in 1849. Both men were to dominate the surveys of the more remote regions of the American West in the 1870s and 1880s.

Powell, a self-taught naturalist and geologist who lost part of an arm in the Civil War, was the professor of geology at Illinois Wesleyan College in 1867 when he organized a party of amateur naturalists to explore the higher peaks in the Colorado Rocky Mountains. He returned the following year with an even larger party which included among its members George Vasey. Educated at Illinois Wesleyan, Vasey helped organize the Illinois Natural History Society and served as its first president. His visit to Colorado spurred an interest in the grass family which he carried to the end of his life, for in 1872 he became a curator of botany at the Smithsonian Institution. Watson and Vasey described most of the new species Powell and his group found, several of which were gathered by his wife, Emma Dean Powell.

When the Powells saw the deep canyons of the Green and Colorado rivers, they realized that this was the last great unexplored region of the United States. From 1869 until 1872, Powell and his associates explored the wilds of the two river canyons, his 1869 boat trip down the Colorado River being one of the most exciting adventures in western American explorations. Powell's 1875 *Explorations of the Colorado River of the west and its tributaries* was filled with the engraved sketches of Frederick Dellenbaugh

*Photography on the American frontier (left) became more common after the Civil War. Timothy O'Sullivan took this photograph on the Truckee River, Nevada, of a boat used during the King expedition in 1867. The pale sky pilot (Polemonium brandegei) (above) was found by Townshend Brandegee who was collecting for the Hayden Survey.*

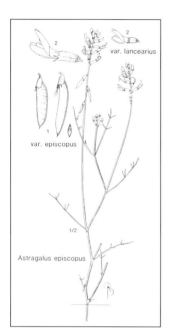

*Astragalus Episcopus (above) as technically illustrated by Bobbi Angell and published in* Intermountain flora *in 1989. The Colorado River (right) photographed by E. O. Beaman in 1871 during Powell's expedition through the Grand Canyon.*

and etchings made from the photographs of John Hillers. In 1869, Powell and his men discovered the last unknown mountain range in the nation which he named the Henry Mountains for the Secretary of the Smithsonian Joseph Henry.

*I*n 1872, Powell's last year in the field, his sister resided in the small, southern Utah, Mormon community of Kanab. Ellen Powell Thompson, generally ignored by the other women of the community, occupied her time collecting plants while her husband, Almon Harris Thompson, explored the Colorado Plateau for Powell. She sent her efforts to Watson who named several of the new species in her honor in an 1873 *American Naturalist* article. The Thompsons remained in the West making observations for Powell until 1877, but their departure from Kanab meant that she stopped making botanical excursions. In 1872, one of Thompson's field assistants, Frank Bishop, found a new species of locoweed which Watson named *Astragalus episcopus* in a play of words on his surname.

Hayden, who had studied medicine and geology with John Newberry, was a professor of geology at the University of Pennsylvania when he began his survey of the western territories in 1867. He was not a newcomer to the West. He collected plants for Lieutenant Governor Kemble Warren from 1855 until 1857 while serving as geologist on an expedition up the Yellowstone River to the mouth of the Big Horn. He also collected when he was surgeon-naturalist for Captain William F. Raynolds who followed the Yellowstone to its source, observing the geological wonders of "Colter's Hell." The few new plants were named by Engelmann in an 1862 article in the *Transactions of the American Philosophical Society.*

When Hayden formed what became known as the "Hayden Survey," he employed a broad array of skilled scientists. Most of the work that dominated his life from 1870 until 1886 was concentrated in the Rocky Mountains. He became interested in dinosaurs and championed the work of Edward Drinker Cope in opposition to Powell's dinosaur expert Othniel Charles Marsh. Marsh's expeditions were largely privately supported, thanks in part to an inheritance from his uncle, financier and philanthropist, George Foster Peabody.

The most important of the many botanists who labored for Hayden was Townshend Stith Brandegee who collected in the high mountains of southern Colorado in 1875. Brandegee would later pioneer botanical explorations in the interior of Baja California. While Watson named several of the new plants he found, Brandegee himself accounted for many in one of Hayden's many published reports.

The surveys of King, Powell, and Hayden differed from those previous in one important way—each employed a photographer. King's photographer was Timothy H. O'Sullivan who had learned the trade from Mathew Brady. He later served on the Wheeler Survey. Powell's photographer was John Hiller who used the wet plate process. It was Hayden's photographer however, who would leave the greatest impression upon the American public with his views of the American West. William Henry Jackson established a studio in Omaha, Nebraska, in 1869. He equipped a wagon and photographed the building of the railroad in Wyoming and Utah, scenic views of the West, and the disappearing Indian people. From 1870 until 1879 he was Hayden's official photographer, gaining access to some of the most remote and wild portions of the Rocky Mountains. In 1873, he photographed Mt. Holy Cross in Colorado. When he moved his studio to Denver in 1879, General William Palmer of the Rio Grande and Western Railroad outfitted a private rail car as a photography studio, which allowed Jackson to travel widely. His photographs of the Royal Gorge remain among his best known.

The Department of Agriculture and the Smithsonian Institution were also interested in the plants of the American West, but their collectors had a different focus from those working for the surveys. Charles Parry, who had worked as naturalist on several of the wagon road surveys in the 1860s, was mainly associated with Agriculture while Edward Palmer collected for the Smithsonian. Both men made several trips into Utah, Arizona, and Mexico, discovering many new species subsequently named by Sereno Watson. Palmer was a fine ethnobotanist and his collections of artifacts and objects represent some of the best ever obtained by a public institution.

The era of the great geological surveys in the 1870s and 1880s was important to the discovery of botanical oddities and added many new names for Gray to consider as he labored on his *Synoptical flora of North America*. In addition to the survey botanists there were a host of others who were collecting across the nation. During the Civil War, President Lincoln

signed into law the Morrill Act of 1862, which provided grants of land for the support of agricultural colleges. Into these new colleges came numerous botanists trained in the classification of plants, as botany was fundamental to the curriculum. Some who found positions in the western universities had been trained by Gray and his followers, but others were self-taught and very independent. Torrey and then Gray so dominated American

systematic botany that no major publication escaped their prior review. Even journal articles devoted to the description of new plant species were often seen by Gray before an editor would order their printing.

This prior review was reasonable in that Gray had access to the largest library and herbarium in North America, and he could quickly review a manuscript and weed out those supposedly new plants that were already known. This was particulary important for even in the 1880s new American plants were being described in European journals. As Gray aged and became more conservative in his view of species, many western-based authors found their papers rejected because Gray claimed the plants had already been described. This brought an immediate response from many who, having seen the plants in the field, knew them to be distinctly different species.

In the forefront of the western rebels was Edward L. Greene. Greene challenged Gray directly, and when Gray died in 1888, he took on Watson and the rest of the "eastern establishment" with a vengeance. Although few in the West tolerated Greene's taxonomy, none objected to his right to express his opinion without prior censorship. Equal to Greene in his verbal abuse of his fellow botanists was the mining engineer-botanist Marcus Eugene Jones. Both Greene and Jones collected in some of the most remote places in the West, often walking or traveling by wagon. Greene and Jones in particular found many narrowly endemic species restricted to a single geological outcrop. To avoid the editorial opinions of others, each man established his own private journal, reporting his new species without any prior evaluation by others.

Asa Gray published two parts of his *Synoptical flora* before his death. His successors at Harvard, Watson and Benjamin Lincoln Robinson, edited and completed two more and announced a third that was never printed. Gray's death was the forerunner of another event: the end of the nation's social frontier. The census of 1890 showed the United States to be populated from coast to coast. The last battle between the European

*Images of Native Americans were often romanticized, whether for a technical report (far left) or to advertise tobacco .*

invaders and Native American people had been fought; gun fights on the street were fading from memory; and it was no longer possible to look out across the Rocky Mountains or the Great Basin without seeing evidence of modern human occupation.

The study of plants was becoming specialized. Few taxonomists knew of all the plants of a state let alone a region or nation. People could not afford to buy the great printed works common in the eighteenth century and copied in the many documents published by the federal government in the nineteenth. Botanical journals became the standard outlet for the description of new plants. The great artists were replaced by skilled illustrators with a concomitant change in style; this in turn gave way to photographers.

The end of the American frontier also saw the end of America's own discovery; the rivers and mountains were known. The forests and soils would be mapped in time, and most of the nation geologically explored. Floras would appear for most of the states, but Torrey and Gray's goal of summarizing the plants of north America north of Mexico remains unfulfilled.

The men and women who labor currently to summarize the plants of North America recognize the contributions made by those who came before. The goal of future generations is to assure that the plants survive.

# Epilogue

I n 1864, Charles Christopher Parry, botanist, was collecting in the Rocky Mountains of Colorado. Before him lay three great peaks all in excess of 14,000 feet. The tallest he named for Asa Gray, the next, only ten feet less, he named for John Torrey, and to the third, slightly lower still, he ascribed George Engelmann's name. Upon each grows *Picea engelmannii*, the Colorado blue spruce, and one cannot walk upon any of them without seeing a plant named by Torrey or Gray. It is a fitting tribute.

Botany since 1890 has fragmented into a myriad of subdisciplines. Even the word "taxonomy" has given way to "systematics" as the identification, classification, and naming of plants has become more experimental. The end of the social frontier in 1890 did not mean that there was an end to new botanical discoveries. Gray's antagonists, Greene and Jones, and others like them such as Per Axel Rydberg, John Kunkel Small, and Amos Arthur Heller, to mention only three, were right in one important way; there were still many new species to be discovered. Botanical explorations became individual efforts, often undertaken with limited support. College professors encouraged their students to collect even if some went no further than the edge of campus to find new species.

Alice Eastwood, a Denver schoolteacher, became an assistant curator of botany at the California Academy of Sciences in 1892. Her adventures in Colorado and Utah, searching for plants while the Wetherill brothers, local ranchers, sought new Indian ruins to match their finds at Mesa Verde, were to be repeated by others who explored the American West. In time, collectors worked in pairs, with Eastwood and John Thomas Howell being one of the first. Their work in California and across the Great Basin to Colorado resulted in the discovery of many rare plants. Their discoveries were exceeded by the efforts of Dwight Ripley and Rupert C. Barneby who, from the late 1930s until the 1950s, found many narrowly endemic species in the West. The efforts of Bassett Maguire and Arthur Holmgren in the 1940s were followed by those of Arthur's son Noel and this writer in the 1960s. Unlike the others who tended to collect on the desert in the spring, we sought those rare plants that flowered in the heat of the summer and early fall when, instead of being in school, we collected plants.

As the 1970s passed into the 1980s it became obvious that the number of truly new American species was declining. The last three new genera and their only species were described in the 1970s: *Apacheria*, *Shoshonia* and *Dedeckera*. All are rare and restricted in their distribution.

The decade of the 1970s saw most plant systematists involved with the environmental movement. When the Endangered Species Act finally included the word "plant" in 1972, much effort was devoted to the rediscovery of those species long unseen. Many were located, but far too

*An 1874 advertisement for raspberries is typical of 19th-century commerical illustrations of agricultrual subjects.*

many were found to have become extinct. The collection of seeds for the growing of rare plants became an important task of modern plant explorers. The discovery that the genetic diversity of agriculturally important plants was often limited resulted in the depressing discovery that older strains of some species were gone, and natural populations of others were rare or unknown. The genetic future of many plants became important, and plant explorers were once again in the field, not searching for the new, but hoping to find the old.

The botanical frontier in the United States closed at the end of 1989, a century after the social frontier had closed. Today, plant explorers must search far beyond the national boundaries of the United States for new plants. The frontier is in the tropics. Modern plant explorers comb the tropical forests of Latin and South America as well as those of Africa and the Old World in search of novelties. Seeds are gathered for botanical gardens, specimens are preserved for the herbarium and chemical analysis, and the new species are described and often illustrated.

In a sense it is no different from the first specimens taken to Europe nearly five centuries ago. Each discovery holds an unknown future. The next one might be the key to finding a cure for a particular type of cancer or AIDS. It might even be the key to unlocking a genetic mystery or the long-sought solution to some puzzle. Then again it might just be pretty.

Imagine the world without its wildflowers, its great conifers, and all that abounds in their midst. Without them there is no life as we understand it.

Generations of men and women have labored to understand what we see around us. This modest work has attempted to tell a bit of their story. It has reported their accomplishments, their disappointments, and their deaths. Yet they live in the history of the plants they found. Old-growth Douglas fir is more than merely the home of the spotted owl or the economic base of a part of the nation. It has a meaning vested in the person of a man, a plant explorer who gave his life that we might better understand this tree, and the forest of which it is a part.

*Seed catalogs (above) have long been popular with the general public, displaying vegetables and flowering trees, shrubs and herbs to herald the coming of each spring. (Left) A 19th-century tobacco label.*

# Bibliography

Allan, M. 1964. *The Tradescants, their plants, gardens and museum, 1570-1662.* London: Michael Joseph.

Allan, M. 1967. *The Hookers of Kew, 1785-1911.* London: Michael Joseph.

Bartlett, R.A. 1962. *Great surveys of the American west.* Norman: University of Oklahoma Press.

Berkeley, E. and D.S. Berkeley. 1963. *John Clayton, pioneer of American botany.* Chapel Hill: University of North Carolina Press.

Berkeley, E. and D.S. Berkeley. 1969. *Dr. Alexander Garden of Charles Town.* Chapel Hill: University of North Carolina Press.

Berkeley, E. and D.S. Berkeley. 1982. *The life and travels of John Bartram; from Lake Ontario to the River St. John.* Tallahassee: Florida University Press.

Blunt, W. and S. Raphael. 1979. *The illustrated herbal.* London: Frances Lincoln Publishers Ltd.

Burrough, R.D. 1961. *The natural history of the Lewis and Clark expedition.* East Lansing: Michigan State University Press.

Coats, A.M. 1970. *The plant hunters: Being a history of the horticultural pioneers, their quests and their discoveries from the Renaissance to the twentieth century.* New York: MacGraw-Hill.

Cutright, P.R. 1969. *Lewis and Clark. Pioneering naturalists.* Urbana: University of Illinois Press.

Dupree, A.H. 1959. *Asa Gray, 1810-1888.* Cambridge: Belknap Press of Harvard University Press.

Ewan, J. 1969. *A short history of botany in the United States.* New York: Hafner Publishing Co.

Ewan, J. and N. Ewan. 1970. *John Banister and his Natural History of Virginia 1678-1692.* Urbana: University of Illinois Press.

Ewan, J. and N. Ewan. 1981. *Biographical dictionary of Rocky Mountain naturalists.* Regnum Veg. 107.

Frick, G.F. and R.P. Stearns. 1961. *Mark Catesby: The colonial Audubon.* Urbana: University of Illinois Press.

Geiser, S.W. [orig. date] 1948. *Naturalists of the frontier.* Reprint [2nd edit.]. Dallas: Southern Methodist University Press.

Goetzmann, W.H. 1959. *Army exploration in the American west, 1803-1863.* New Haven: Yale University Press.

Goetzmann, W.H. 1966. *Exploration and empire.* New York: Knopf.

Goetzmann, W.H. 1986. *New lands, new men. America and the second great age of discovery.* New York: Viking.

Graustein, J.E. 1967. *Thomas Nuttall, naturalist; explorations in America, 1808-1841.* Cambridge: Harvard University Press.

Henrey, B. 1975. *British botanical and horticultural literature before 1800.* 3 vols. London: Oxford University Press.

Humphrey, H.B. 1961. *Makers of North American botany.* New York: The Ronald Press Co.

Jackson, D. 1962. *Letters of the Lewis and Clark expedition and related documents, 1783-1854.* Norman: University of Oklahoma Press.

Jackson, D. and M.E. Spence. 1970. *The expeditions of John Charles Frémont.* Vol. 1. Urbana: University of Illinois Press.

Jackson, W.T. 1965. *Wagon roads west: A study of federal road surveys and constructions in the trans-Mississippi west, 1846-1869.* New Haven: Yale University Press.

Lemmon, K. 1968. *The golden age of plant hunters.* London: Phoenix House Publications.

McKelvey, S.D. 1955. *Botanical exploration of the trans-Mississippi west, 1790-1850.* Jamaica Plains: Arnold Arboretum.

McVaugh, R. 1956. *Edward Palmer, plant explorer of the American west.* Norman: University of Oklahoma Press.

Morwood, W. 1973. *Traveler in a vanished landscape. The life and times of David Douglas, botanical explorer.* New York: Clarkson N. Potter, Inc.

Reed, H.S. 1942. *A short history of the plant sciences.* Waltham: Chronica Botanica Company.

Reveal, J.L., G.F. Frick, C.R. Broome and M.L. Brown. 1987. Botanical explorations and discoveries in colonial Maryland. *Huntia* 7.

Rodgers, A.D. III. 1942. *John Torrey; a story of North American botany.* Princeton: Princeton University Press.

Ross, P.L. 1984. *The John Tradescants, gardeners to the rose and lily queen.* London: Peter Owen.

Savage, H. Jr. and E.J. Savage. 1986. *André and François-André Michaux.* Charlottesville: University of Virginia Press.

Spence, M.E. and D. Jackson. 1973. *The expeditions of John C. Frémont.* Vol. 2. Urbana: University of Illinois Press.

Stafleu, F.A. 1971. Linnaeus and the Linnaeans; the spreading of their ideas in systematic botany. *Regnum Veg.* 79.

Stearns, R.P. 1970. *Science in the British colonies of America.* Urbana: University of Illinois Press.

Webber, R. 1968. *The early horticulturalists.* Newton Abbot: David and Charles.

# *Index*

## *A*

Acosta, J., 12-13
Aristotle, 9, 12
Arnott, G.W., 99, 105, 120
Audubon, J., 126, 128

## *B*

Baldwin, W., 112-114
Banister, J., 25-26, 29-30, 75, 82
Banks, J., 81, 87, 89, 92
Barclay, G., 121, 123
Barton, B.S., 71-72, 74-75,
  77-79, 81, 113, 115
Barton, W.P.C., 80, 82
Bartram, J., 42, 49, 50, 53-55, 58,
  60-62, 68, 74-75, 82
Bartram, W., 49, 53, 58, 60-62,
  68, 74-75, 82, 114
Bauhin, C., 19, 34, 39
Beckwith, E., 141-142
Beechey, W., 99-101, 105, 120
Bentham, G., 123, 143, 150
Bigelow, J., 138, 141
Botta, P.E., 103
Brackenridge, W.D., 123
Bradbury, J., 78-81, 112
Brandegee, T.S., 151-152
Brewer, W.H., 146
Bridges, T., 146-147
Brunfels, O., 14
Burman, J., 39
Burser, J., 19

## *C*

Canbdolle, A.P., 105, 115, 143,
  150
Carrington, J., 142
Carson, C., 125, 129, 130, 131
Catesby, M., 7, 37, 39-42, 49, 55,
  57-58, 60, 75, 82
Clark, W., 67, 71-72, 77-78, 80-
  82, 93-94, 100-101, 111-112, 115
Clayton, J., 30, 39-42, 44, 46,
  49-50, 53, 58, 61-62, 65, 120
Clifford, G., 39-41
Colden, C., 53-54, 58
Colden, J., 58, 60
Collie, A., 100
Collignon, J.-N., 87
Collinson, P., 29, 39-40, 42, 44,
  49-50, 53, 54-55, 60-62
Compton, H., 25, 29-30
Cook, J., 81, 89, 100
Cornut, J.P., 19
Coulter, T., 105-107, 132
Cruezefeldt, F., 141

## *D*

Dale, S., 37, 39
Dana, J.D., 123, 146
Darwin, C., 144
Dillenius, J.J., 34, 37, 39-40, 50, 53
Dioscorides, 13-14, 16
Dodoens, R., 16
Don, D., 107
Doody, S., 26, 29-30
Douglas, D., 71, 85-87, 89, 92-
  94, 96-97, 99-100, 102-103,
  105-107, 109, 116, 118, 120,
  123, 131, 135, 157
Drummond, T., 89, 93, 116, 120
Dunbar, W., 111
Durand, E., 142

## *E*

Eastwood, A., 156
Eaton, A., 113, 115, 148
Eaton, D.C., 148
Ehret, G.D., 7, 21, 42, 60-61, 65
Elliott, S., 113-114
Emory, W.H., 131-132, 138-139,
  141, 148
Engelmann, G., 126, 131-132,
  138-139, 141, 144, 152, 156
Eschscholtz, J.F., 102-103, 129
Evelyn, J., 22

## *F*

Fendler, A., 132, 138
Franklin, B., 44, 55, 58, 60-62
Freeman, T., 111
Frémont, J.C., 124-126, 128-133,
  135-136, 138, 141-142, 148
Fuchs, L., 16, 19

## *G*

Gairdner, M., 119, 128
Gambel, W., 130, 135
Garden, A., 58, 60-62
Gerard, J., 14, 16, 19, 22
Gesner, K. von, 16
Geyer, K.A., 124, 126, 128
Gordon, A., 126, 128
Gray, A., 120-121, 123-126, 128,
  130, 132, 135-136, 138, 141-
  144, 147-148, 150-151, 153-156

## *G*

Greene, E.L., 154, 156
Gregg, J., 132, 138
Gronovius, J.F., 39-40, 42, 44, 53,
  60-62, 65
Gunnison, J., 141, 146

## *H*

Haenke, T., 86, 92
Halsteed, W., 37
Harford, W.G.W., 146
Hariot, J., 16, 25
Hartweg, K.T., 131
Harvey, W.H., 132
Hayden, F.V., 151-153
Heermann, A.L., 142
Heller, A.A., 156
Hilgard, E., 142
Hill, J., 61
Hinds, R.B., 121, 123
Holmgren, A.H., 156
Holmgren, N.H., 156.
Hooker, W.J., 97, 99-100, 103,
  105-107, 109, 116, 120, 123,
  126, 128, 136, 138, 147
Hosack, D., 74, 82, 113
Howell, J.T., 156

## *I*

Ives, J.C., 143
James, E., 111-114, 150
Jefferson, T., 65, 67-68, 70-72, 75,
  77-78, 82, 111-112

## *J*

Jeffrey, J., 146
Jones, H., 22, 29-30, 37, 58
Jones, M.E., 154, 156
Josselyn, J., 25
Jussieu, A. de, 70, 87

## *K*

Kalm, P., 54-55, 57
Kearney, S.W., 131-133
Kellogg, A., 136, 146
Kern, E.M., 131, 139
Kern, R., 139, 141
King, C., 147-148, 151-152
Kotzebue, O. von, 101-102
Krieg, D., 29-30

## *L*

Lamarck, J.B. de, 67, 87
Lambert, A., 74, 81, 92, 97, 136
Langsdorff, H. von, 101-102
Lawson, J., 37, 39
L'Ecluse, C. de, 12, 16

Lewis, M., 67, 71-72, 74-75, 77-78, 80-82, 93-94, 100-101, 111-112, 115
Lhwyd, E., 29
Lindley, J., 97, 105-106, 136
Linnaeus, C., 19, 30, 33-34, 39-40, 42, 44-46, 49-50, 53-55, 57-58, 60-61, 65, 67, 75, 87, 100, 115, 120
Lisa, M., 77-80
Lobb, W., 90, 135-136, 147
L'Obel, M. de, 14, 16
Long, S.H., 112, 113
Lord, J., 37
Lüders, F.G.F., 126, 128
Lyon, J., 74-75

### M

Macomb, J.M., 143
Malaspina, A., 86, 89
Maguire, B., 156
Marcy, R., 139
Marshall, H., 53, 58, 75, 94
Martyn, J., 29, 50
McLeod, A., 93-94, 96
Menzies, A., 87, 89-90, 92, 94, 100, 105, 109, 136
Michaux, A., 67-68, 70, 74, 77, 82, 113, 115, 120
Michaux, F.A., 68, 70, 72, 75
Mitchell, J., 44-46, 49, 54-55
Mitchell, S.L., 77, 113, 115
M'Mahon, B., 75, 114
Moçiño, J.M., 89-90
Monardes, N.B., 12
Morison, R., 25-26, 34, 45
Muhlenberg, G.H., 75

### N

Née, L., 86
Newberry, J.S., 142-143, 152
Nicollet, J.N., 124, 130
Nicolson, F., 29-30, 37
Nuttall, T., 74-75, 77-82, 112-121, 126, 130

### O

Oviedo y Valdés, G.F. de, 11-13

### P

Palmer, E., 153
Parke, J.G., 141-142
Parkinson, J., 14, 16, 22, 49
Parry, C.C., 138, 153, 156
Parry, E., 93
Patten, H., 142
Petiver, J., 29-30, 34, 37, 39, 53
Pike, Z.M., 111-112, 130
Plukenet, L., 26, 30, 34, 45
Poinsett, J.R., 124
Pope, J., 141-142
Powell, J.W., 151-152
Pursh, F., 67, 71, 74-75, 77-78, 81-82, 90, 92, 99-100, 105, 113, 115, 120

### R

Rafinesque-Schmalz, C.S., 77, 79, 115, 121, 142
Ray, J., 25-26, 30, 37, 42, 45
Raynolds, W.F., 152
Redouté, P.J., 62, 65, 70, 72
Rémy, E.J., 146
Richard, L.C., 70
Richardson, J., 93, 99
Ridgeway, R., 148
Ripley, D., 156
Robin, J., 14, 19
Robin, V., 14, 19
Roscoe, W., 79, 81
Rothrock, J.T., 151
Rudbeck, O., 54
Rydberg, P.A., 156

### S

Sabine, J., 97
Sargent, C.S., 151
Say, T., 112, 114-115, 123
Schoolcraft, H.R., 114
Schweinitz, L.D. von, 114
Scouler, J., 99-100
Sessé y Lacasta, M. de, 90
Sherard, W., 34, 37, 39
Short, C.W., 114
Simpson, J.H., 139, 143-144
Sitgreaves, L., 139, 141

Sloane, H., 30, 34, 37, 39-40, 54, 58
Small, J.K., 156
Smith, J.E., 30, 92
Snyder, J.A., 141
Spalding, H.H., 128
Sprague, I., 123, 128, 138
Stansbury, H., 139, 141-142
Steller, G., 86-87, 101

### T

Theophrastos, 9, 13
Thompson, E.P., 152
Thurber, G., 138, 143
Torrey, J., 113-116, 119-121, 124-126, 129-130, 132-133, 135-136, 138-139, 141-144, 150, 154-156
Tournefort, J.P. de, 45-46
Townsend, J.K., 116-119
Tradescant, J., 19, 25, 44
Turner, W., 16

### V

Vancouver, G., 89-90, 92
Vasey, G., 151
Vernon, W., 29-30
Vosnesensky, I.G., 123

### W

Walter, T., 54, 75, 81
Warren, G.K., 152
Watson, S., 148, 150-155
Wheeler, G.M., 151
Whipple, A.W., 141, 146
Whitman, M., 128
Whitney, J.D., 144, 146-147
Wilkes, C., 123
Willdenow, C.L., 75
Williams, H., 37
Williamson, R.S., 142
Wislizenus, F.A., 131-132
Woodhouse, S., 139
Wrangel, F.P., 123
Wright, C., 138
Wyeth, N., 116-119

### Y

Young, W., 60, 62